# EBOLA

*FROM OUTBREAK TO CRISIS TO CONTAINMENT*

**By The Associated Press**

Mango Media
Miami
in collaboration with
The Associated Press

AP Editions
Copyright © 2015 The Associated Press

Published by Mango Media, Inc.
www.mangomedia.us

This is a work of non-fiction adapted from articles and content by
journalists of The Associated Press and published with permission.

**Ebola** *From Outbreak to Crisis to Containment*
**ISBN**: 978-1-63353-040-9

## Publisher's Note

AP Editions are a collection of reports written by staff members of The Associated Press.

These stories are presented in their original form and are intended to provide a snapshot of history as the moments occurred.

We hope you enjoy these selections from the front lines of newsgathering.

"This is not a problem that's going to go away any time soon."

- President Barack Obama, December 12, 2014

# Table of Contents

# Overview

Strands of the Ebola virus have been around since the late 70s. In that time, over 21,000 people have died. The worst outbreak in history began in the spring of 2014 in West Africa. This current strand of the virus is responsible for over 8,000 deaths in the past 11 months.

Five countries have suffered the most: Liberia, Guinea, Mali, Nigeria, and Sierra Leone. To this day, the World Health Organization fears that the reported cases of infected and dead are slim compared to the actual tolls.

As the world fights to contain the outbreak, follow the origin and path of this devastating disease with the on-location reporting and analysis of The Associated Press.

# Introduction

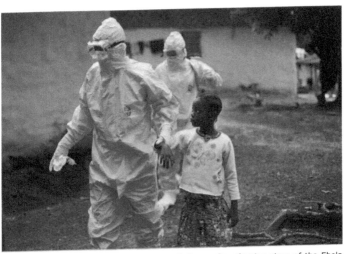

Nine-year-old Nowa Paye is taken to an ambulance after showing signs of the Ebola infection in the village of Freeman Reserve, about 30 miles north of Monrovia, Liberia, September 30, 2014. (AP Photo/Jerome Delay, File)

### A Constant Threat
Monrovia, Liberia
October 3, 2014
By Krista Larson

The nurse excitedly grabbed the sheet of paper with 11-year-old Chancey's lab results. "It's negative, it's negative," she shouted above the sound of her boots pounding the gravel as she ran toward the outdoor Ebola ward.

Soon the boy in a neon green T-shirt came running to the hole in the orange plastic fencing to greet her. The barrier separates health workers from those sick with one of the world's deadliest diseases.

"We're so glad he's going to make it. His little brothers will really need him now — their mother just died last night," a nurse told me.

Instantly that moment of rare joy amid Liberia's Ebola epidemic turned to sorrow, and I could no longer make eye contact with the beaming boy. Knowing that he did not yet know his mother was dead — and I did — was just too much.

Residents of the St. Paul Bridge neighborhood wearing personal protective equipment, take a man suspected of carrying the Ebola virus to the Island Clinic in Monrovia, Liberia, September 28, 2014. (AP Photo/Jerome Delay, File)

Here in Liberia, more than 2,000 people have lost their lives to a disease that shows no mercy, and even the stories of survivors are tainted with unspeakable loss. Radio talk shows describe infants trying to breastfeed off dead mothers, orphans whose relatives are so afraid of contagion that they refuse to take in brokenhearted children.

For months I had pored over situation reports from the World Health Organization and listened to experts describe the possibility of a disaster beyond measure as the Ebola epidemic gathered speed. Nothing prepares you, though, for the heartbreak and the fear now ravaging Liberia.

———

Krista Larson, an Associated Press correspondent based in Dakar, Senegal, arrived in Monrovia on Sept. 25, 2014 to join AP staff covering the Ebola epidemic. Here she describes some of her experiences.

———

Friends and family had begged me not to go. A housekeeper cried as I left for the airport and gave me a crucifix that she told me not to take it off even though I am not a Catholic. Even my assistant at the plastic baggage wrap station in the steamy overcrowded airport at midnight was sure this was all just some horrible mix-up. "Liberia? You mean Nigeria? You know people are dying there!"

The dangers of covering this story were brought home Thursday with word that Ashoka Mukpo, an American freelance cameraman who had just taken a job in Liberia with NBC, was diagnosed with Ebola and is scheduled to return to the U.S. for treatment.

After meeting my colleagues in Morocco, we embarked on a flight full of other journalists and aid workers for Liberia on one of the last commercial airlines still servicing the country.

We arrived in Monrovia at 3 a.m. in a thunderstorm, and after a sleepless flight, we washed our hands in a mixture of bleach and water for the first time and had our temperatures taken before we picked up the soggy luggage that was not lost by our airline. Rainy season in sub-Saharan Africa is always a sweaty endeavor, and it takes every bit of self-discipline to avoid touching your face to wipe the sweat from your brow.

Ebola is spread only through direct contact with the bodily fluids of people showing symptoms of the disease. That said, people have fallen sick after coming into contact with soiled linens. Vigorous hand-washing is the mainstay of Ebola prevention, though at this point it's nearly impossible to know who is sick with Ebola and who might just have malaria or the flu.

The Ebola patients I saw lined up outside the clinic my first day of reporting were not bleeding from the eyes — we're told that actually happens only in a minority of cases. Instead, we found a very weak and tired boy, and I winced at the sight of his mother touching his sweaty face with her bare hands. It might only be a matter of time before she too becomes sick.

It's hard to forget the reason why we are in Monrovia: When you make a call with a local phone number a public service message reminds you "Ebola is real!" before the call goes through. The wailing of ambulance sirens is constant, and men can be seen pushing the sick in wheelbarrows when no such emergency vehicle is available.

I'm here as part of a team of AP reporters including photographers Jerome Delay and Abbas Dulleh, video producer Andrew Drake, correspondent Jonathan Paye-Layleh and television contributor Wade Williams, who fearlessly interviews Ebola victims with her warm, commanding voice.

"Wear long sleeves and don't touch anyone," she said firmly as I prepared to get out of her car and visit an Ebola clinic for the first time last week. "And leave your bag in the car."

I admit I was initially afraid to come to Liberia. Unlike the wars and coups I have covered, you cannot see or avoid Ebola as you can a fighter. If you are shot, you know to seek medical attention immediately. Ebola's incubation period, by contrast, is up to 21 days. Every sore throat, every achy muscle can set off anxiety.

And yet the world needs to know what is happening here: Ebola is obliterating entire neighborhoods, leaving orphaned children with no one to lean on but a tree.

More and more international journalists are starting to come. Several dozen working for outlets ranging from American newspapers to European radio are now taking Liberia's story to an ever-widening audience.

Aid workers in West Africa say they need more than just gloves and supplies. They need more people willing to come here despite the personal risks. The anguish and pain are too much for Liberia to bear alone.

# 1

# The Beginning

Kinkasa Julien, whose mother died of the Ebola virus and her sister the week before, crouches in a cemetery behind the Kikwit, Zaire hospital and weeps next to her sister's grave, May 26, 1995. (AP Photo/David Guttenfelder)

### Ebola Virus Blamed; City Quarantined
Kinshasa, Zaire
May, 10 1995
By The Associated Press

A discoverer of the deadly Ebola virus said a mysterious disease that has killed more than 100 people in Zaire has all the hallmarks of Ebola, but he could not confirm the virus was responsible.

The 600,000 residents of Kikwit were placed under quarantine after an un-identified illness began sweeping the city, 375 miles east of Kinshasa, the capital, in mid-April. Ebola is suspected but has not been verified.

Dr. Peter Piot, the new head of the U.N. AIDS program, co-discovered the Ebola virus in 1976 when he was working in Zaire. He told The Associated

Press in Geneva that he could not confirm the recent outbreak in Zaire was Ebola but he said it has all the characteristics of it.

As with Ebola, the illness reported in Zaire caused fevers and deadly hemorrhaging, with blood coming out of victims' ears and eyes, he said. In Belgium, the international medical aid group Doctors Without Borders said a second city may also have an outbreak of Ebola.

The group has reports that at least 10 people in Mosango, 75 miles west of Kikwit, have been infected with a disease believed to be Ebola, spokeswoman Gerda Bossier said. Three of the 10 have died. The group has sent a team to Zaire to investigate. An order of nuns based in Bergamo, Italy, said two sisters died in the past two weeks in Kikwit, where they worked as nurses. Two other members of the order were sick and in serious but stable condition at a Kikwit hospital, according to a statement from the Poverelle order north of Milan. The order did not describe the nuns' symptoms.

Two sisters of one of the nuns, on their return to Italy after the funeral, were placed under observation in a hospital isolation ward as a precaution, a spokesman at Riuniti Hospital in Bergamo said.

Seven Zairean and four other Italian members of the Poverelle order worked at the hospital in Kikwit but do not show signs of the disease that killed the two nuns, the order said. People who develop Ebola become ill one week after infection and die one week later, Piot said.

Ebola's ferocity has given it notoriety - it was the virus fought in the movie "Robin Cook's 'Virus,'" which appeared Monday on NBC-TV. The recent movie "Outbreak" concerned a hemorrhagic virus that first appeared in Zaire, although it was not specifically named as Ebola. And the best-selling book "The Hot Zone" by Richard Preston focused on an outbreak of a strain of the Ebola virus among monkeys outside Washington.

Ebola was considered the most deadly virus before the appearance of HIV, which causes AIDS. Ebola kills about 90 percent of those it infects and there is no treatment or vaccine. It is spread through body fluids and secretions, though not through casual contact. Previous Ebola outbreaks were caused by poor hospital hygiene, Piot said. Ebola is unlikely to reach epidemic proportions because of improved precautions, he said.

Two WHO specialists set out for Zaire on Tuesday, and the U.S. Centers for Disease Control and Prevention said it was sending a team of investigators equipped with protective suits and respirators.

"With the little we know, we're going to have to assume that this could be Biosafety Level 4," the highest level of possible infection, said Dr. Rima Khabbaz, an infectious disease specialist at the CDC.

Investigators hope to reach Kikwit in a few days and the diagnosis should be relatively rapid "if it's something we know and have dealt with," Khabbaz said. CDC experts were analyzing victims' blood samples that arrived from Zaire on Monday - a process that could take up to 72 hours, CDC spokesman

Bob Howard said. In 1976, 274 of 300 people died in an Ebola outbreak in one Zairean village. There have also been outbreaks in southern Sudan and one confirmed case this year in Ivory Coast, Piot said. Officials at Zaire's health ministry say the outbreak in Kikwit began April 10 when a surgical patient at Kikwit's hospital contaminated medical personnel.

Sixty-three people remained hospitalized there Tuesday with the illness.

### Rooted in Africa
Kinshasa, Zairean
May 10, 1995
By The Associated Press

Two children wait outside the hospital at Kikwit, Zaire, where a deadly Ebola virus killed dozens. The children were waiting for the body of a relative reported killed by the disease. They covered their faces in an effort to protect themselves from the virus. A U.S. govenment task force reports at least 29 previously unknown diseases, such as the Ebola virus and AIDS, have appeared since 1973 around the world, May 12, 1995. (AP Photo/Jean-Marc Bouju)

Medical experts from the United States have arrived in the Zairean city of Kikwit, to begin work on containing the virulent disease Ebola. The medical team were accompanied by a group of journalists who had been given special permission by the Zairean authorities to enter the area. Amongst them was an AP photographer who has provided one of the first pictures to come out of the stricken city. A quarantine zone of 190 kilometers (120 miles) now stretches around the town of Kikwit. Its 600,000 inhabitants have been ordered to stay indoors and schools and health clinics have been shut down.

Pat Galloway, a registered nurse and training assistant in the Office of Health and Safety at the Centers for Disease Control and Prevention in Atlanta, poses in a field protective suit and respirator, like ones researchers will use when investigating cases of Ebola virus infection in Zaire. A team of researchers from the CDC have joined with the World Health Orginization to investigate the virus outbreak in the African nation. The respirator consists of a battery powered, filtered intake, hose and hood that creates a positive air flow inside the hood blowing out holes in the chin area. It is the main line of defense researchers will have against infection, May 11, 1995. (AP Photo/Tannen Maury)

In addition to cases in Kikwit, there have been outbreaks in the villages of Mosango and Yassa Bonga, and perhaps in a fourth village - Kenge - halfway between Kikwit and the capital, Kinshasa.

On Friday a team of medics from the US Centers for Disease Control and Prevention arrived in Kikwit from Atlanta, to find a means of containing the disease.

Ebola's symptoms are similar to those of malaria - sufferers usually complain of headaches and fever.

But it's then followed by severe diarrhea and vomiting. In 80% of cases death follows within days as blood pours from the bodies of the victims.

According to the World Health Organization at least 48 people have died and 17 more have been hospitalized.

Medical experts have urged people to stay calm and not to panic. The focus of efforts now is to stop the virus spreading.

Zambian President, Frederick Chiluba told a press conference at the South African Summit, that measures would be taken to keep Ebola out of his country.

"First we're happy that medical people have rushed in to try and contain the situation, and I am sure that we will be as a country taking a precautionary and preventative measures to stop that outbreak - getting into Zambia that is." - Zambian President Frederick Chiluba

But for the people of Kikwit the suffering, fear and confusion goes on.

This exclusive photograph, one of the first from the afflicted region and taken by the Associated Press, reflects the desperate measures which people are taking to protect themselves.

These two boys have lost a relative to Ebola. They've been ordered to ignore their cultural traditions and not to touch or wash the corpse.

As they wait anxiously in the cemetery, they cover their faces with their clothes in the hope that this gesture will shield them from the disease.

Nobody has told them that their action won't make any difference.

A woman suffering from bloody diarrhea, headache and high fever, the classic signs of Ebola, waits at the emergency ward of the Kikwit General Hospital, 250 miles southeast of Kinshasa, May 17, 1995. (AP Photo/Jean-Marc Bouju)

## Failing to Control
Kikwit, Zaire
May 16, 1995
By The Associated Press

The World Health Organization (WHO) announced in Zaire on Tuesday, May 5, 1995 that 77 people of the 84 confirmed cases of the deadly Ebola virus had died. While there have been no confirmed cases of the disease in the capital, Kinshasa, hospital workers are preparing for the possible arrival of victims. Authorities have warned that the lack of observance of quarantine around the diseased town of Kikwit has increased the chances of an outbreak of Ebola in Kinshasa, a sprawling city of 6 million. America's Infectious Diseases Control Centre in Atlanta is continuing to assist in the monitoring of the epidemic. The Zairean Health Minister Doctor Mbumb Mussong announced on Tuesday that he is taking charge of operations to control the epidemic. Doctor Mussong held extensive briefings in Kinshasa with overseas and domestic aid workers and said he was preparing to take an official press party into Kikwit on Wednesday, May 17, 1995.

As of May 22, 1995 American medical experts have been assisting in the search for a cure for a deadly disease which has claimed scores of victims in Zaire. The prime suspect is a virus called Ebola which has struck before in Zaire. In 1976, it infected 300 people in a region near the Ebola river, killing

274 of them. The symptoms begin with severe headaches, followed by diarrhea and bleeding from the eyes, nose and ears. A medical team from Doctors without Borders was sent to Kikwit, a city of 600,000, where the same symptoms had been reported. Fear of the disease was causing panic in the city. From Kikwit, the disease spread to a second city, Mosango. It's believed it was carried there by one of two Italian nuns who had been treating people with the disease in Kikwit. Both nuns have since died. At the Centre for Disease control in Atlanta -- which is analysing blood samples taken from Zaire -- the experts admit they have little idea how the virus spreads.

Ebola is considered to be so lethal that scientists studying the virus at the U.S. Army Research Institute are required to wear respirators and special suits. It has been speculated that the virus spreads through bodily fluids. Many of those infected are doctors and nurses working in a hospital where virus carriers underwent surgery and passed it on to the medical staff.

## Caught Before it Could Spread
Washington
April 20, 1996
By Lauran Neergaard

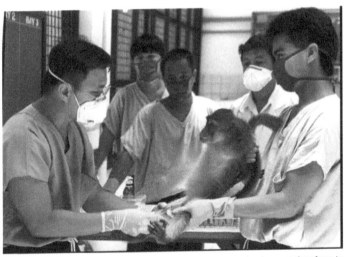

Filipino veterinary doctors extract blood from a macaque monkey in a monkey farm in Tanay, east of Manila, for testing of possible Ebola virus infection. Some 7,000 monkeys in this farm are being tested for possible virus infections under the supervision of experts from the U.S. Center for Disease Control and Preventions (CDC) after a primate center in Texas traced a shipment from the Philippines of monkeys found positive with the Ebola virus, May 1, 1996. (AP Photo/Pat Roque)

Say the word Ebola, and most Americans think of the movie "Outbreak," where one cute little monkey spread a horrific, Ebola-like killer.

No wonder three Ebola-stricken monkeys in remote Alice, Texas, spawned a media circus last week, with helicopters likely terrifying the healthy monkeys as they buzzed over the primate cages at HRP Inc.

Fortunately, Hollywood's not real life. In real life, monkeys are quarantined so sickness is caught before society is at risk - and in Texas, the system worked.

"It's a little bit natural for people to be afraid," said Tony Perez, quarantine chief at the Centers for Disease Control and Prevention. "It certainly is our responsibility to get a clear message out to the public that we really think all the safeguards we have in place are working."

Monkeys are big business, a crucial arm of the $ 500 million industry that supplies almost 2 million animals, from rabbits to chimpanzees, for U.S. biomedical research each year.

Some 55,113 primates were used in 1994 in medical research, from behavioral studies to vaccine testing. More than 18,000 live at seven federally financed primate centers that breed almost all their monkeys in-house.

The rest come from companies that either privately breed primates, which are not indigenous to the United States, or import them from the Philippines, Indonesia or China. A March shipment of 100 rhesus macaques from the Philippines sparked the Texas scare. HRP, which sells 3,000 primates a year and is licensed to handle the riskiest species, followed federal rules to quarantine the animals for 31 days.

While in quarantine, one monkey died, and federal scientists quickly diagnosed Ebola. A second monkey got sick and was destroyed, as were 47 of its monkey neighbors a few days later, to be safe. The other 50 monkeys were quarantined separately, and are being tested to see if they escaped Ebola.

The Texas virus is almost identical to the strain that struck a Reston, Va., primate center in 1989 - good news because that strain is thought probably harmless to people. Four Reston workers exposed to it never got sick.

Ebola found in the wild, in contrast, makes 80 percent of its victims bleed to death. Last year, 245 of the 316 people infected in Zaire died. Ebola also killed 13 people in Gabon in western Africa earlier this year. Importing monkeys will always be risky. African green monkeys, rhesus macaques and cynomolgus monkeys particularly are prone to Ebola-type viruses. But there simply aren't enough monkeys bred in the United States to satisfy the demand from pharmaceutical companies, labs and medical schools.

And those three species are vital, particularly the rhesus that National Institutes of Health primate expert Leo Whitehair calls the "universal model" for all kinds of diseases.

Jonas Salk brewed the first polio vaccine from rhesus monkeys, and the Food and Drug Administration still uses a special rhesus colony isolated on a South Carolina island to test the safety of today's polio shots. But after Reston, the CDC issued new rules to guard against infections.

Of 27 licensed primate importers, the CDC allows 14 to import the three riskiest species. In 1990 and 1991, the CDC made importers test for Ebola every monkey imported of those species. But when no cases were found, it mandated testing just of sick monkeys. The CDC ensures all imported monkeys are transported in quarantine once they're flown over the border, and does surprise inspections to ensure the quarantine centers are run properly.

The question is how healthy the primates are before getting here. The Philippines last week banned all exports until it investigates its primate breeding farms, including the Manila company that shipped both the Texas and Reston monkeys. But the people most at risk - the handlers and scientists who risk bites as they touch monkeys and who breathe the primates' air - say they aren't particularly worried. The system caught Ebola.

"I would not be concerned if I lived near" HRP, Whitehair said. "I know these people and I know they're very, very careful people. They know how to handle this kind of thing."

## History Repeats Itself
Goma, Congo
Sept. 9, 2012
By Melanie Gouby

A medical worker from the U.S. Centers for Disease Control and Prevention, researchers who are working on the Ebola outbreak in Uganda, works at their laboratory in Entebbe 42kms (29 miles) from the capital Kampala, August 2, 2012. (AP Photo/Stephen Wandera)

In September of 2012 The United Nations said that an outbreak of the Ebola virus had killed 31 people in northeastern Congo, more than doubling the death toll from earlier in the year. The U.N. World Health Organization said Friday, September 14, 2012 that there had been 69 cases in all including nine confirmed by a lab.

The Ebola virus has no cure and is deadly in 40 percent to 90 percent of cases. The disease causes severe internal bleeding.

A review of earlier cases has shown that 31 people have died since the beginning of the epidemic in May 2012. More than half of the deaths occurred before August 17, when the Ebola outbreak was officially declared by medical authorities.

Congo has had eight previous Ebola epidemics the first discovery of the virus in 1976.

# 2

# Bushmeat Trade

Mbuti girl Tunduoloki Harriet excitedly holds up a forest antelope caught by a male relative in the Okapi Wildlife Reserve outside the town of Epulu, Congo. The pygmies' traditional practice of hunting bushmeat has devolved into an all-out commercial endeavor - staged not for subsistence, but to feed growing regional markets. The result: the forests, those that remain, are growing emptier by the day, March 21, 2010. (AP Photo/Rebecca Blackwell)

Apes
Africa
February 26, 1998
By The Associated Press

The great apes of Africa are under renewed threat as a result of an explosion in the bushmeat trade fuelled by the logging practices of European companies. According to a report by the Ape Alliance, the largely illegal trade in bushmeat, which includes endangered species, has now developed into a major commercial activity threatening the survival of gorillas, chimpanzees and bonobos (pygmy chimps). Many other species are also threatened, including the forest elephant and dwarf crocodile. The report finds that a rapidly growing timber industry is largely to blame. Ignoring the warnings of conservationists, European logging companies been destroying the apes' habitat. (45% of forest has been lost and 95% is unprotected).

The bushmeat trade has dangers for humans also. Dangerous diseases such as the deadly Ebola virus can be transmitted via ape meat.

The clearing of forests across Africa is being blamed for the increase in the illegal trade in ape meat.

Some conservation groups say that clearances such as these in the West African state of Gabon encourage hunters into previously remote regions to hunt apes.

Leading conservation groups have now joined forces to fight against the trade.

The "Ape Alliance" is a coalition of 34 international organizations and ape specialists taking action to save the great apes - the chimpanzee, gorilla, bonobo and orangutan.

Entitled, "The African Bushmeat Trade -- A Recipe for Extinction", the report said that many other species are also at risk, including the giant pangolin, forest elephant and dwarf crocodile.

It claims to have evidence that directly implicates European timber companies in the trade.

And it is claimed that an increase in activity of Asian logging companies threatens to make the situation worse.

Loggers allegedly supplement their income by hunting wild animals with traps and shotguns and use logging trucks for transport from the forest to the bush markets.

"Over the past several years we have been studying the growth in the commercial trade in bushmeat in Africa. That is meat from wild animals, usually endangered species such as gorillas, chimpanzees, and forest elephants and there is a very alarming trend that this trade is escalating rapidly. This happening because of the growth of the timber industry in the forests of Africa which is allowing people to get immediate access into what were once very remote regions." - Jonathan Pearce, World Society for the Protection of Animals

The Ape Alliance is asking all retailers and consumers of timber to make sure they only buy timber and timber products from forests which have been independently certifies as environmentally responsible.

The Ape Alliance has also asked timber companies to adopt a bushmeat code of conduct and is calling on the E-U to encourage all European timber companies in Africa to adopt this code.

## Bushmeat in Modern Times
Kenya
July 12, 2007
By The Associated Press

Two Allen's swamp monkeys sit in a tree at the Ituri Forest exhibit at the San Diego Zoo, in San Diego. The swamp monkeys were rescued by the zoo from being sold in the illegal bushmeat trade in the Democratic Republic of Congo, May 9, 2006. (AP Photo/Denis Poroy)

Kenyan police have recovered more than 200 kilograms (450 pounds) of "bushmeat" in an unrefrigerated minibus travelling from a wildlife dispersal area outside Nairobi National Park, Kenya Wildlife Service said.

Kenyan authorities said the Zebra and Wildebeest meat was being taken to a market in Nairobi where the driver of the van planned to sell the meat off as beef.
"This meat that was intercepted was not inspected and it was being transported at a very odd hour at four thirty a.m.," confirmed Florence Kulecho, Senior Warden Nairobi National Park.

Three people were arrested in the incident and were charged with poaching and illegal trade in wildlife meat.

Authorities said similar shipments of meat have been entering Nairobi nearly every day for the past two months.

The meat is often illegally slaughtered and posed grave threats from diseases such as Ebola and anthrax linked to eating the flesh of infected animals.

Outside the Meat Training Institute in Nairobi, Kulecho explained the dangers of un-inspected meat.

"It was carried unhygenically and was bound to have diseases such as anthrax and many more. So we want people not to eat meat that is not inspected," she said.

Human outbreaks of Ebola, a deadly virus that causes massive hemorrhaging, have been linked to handling carcasses and eating the flesh of wild animals infected with the disease.

Anthrax and the hemorrhagic disease Rift Valley fever are also risks to people who are exposed to dead infected animals or eat tissue from infected animals.

In many West and Central African countries, bushmeat particularly from primates and elephants is considered a delicacy.

But in Kenya, the main reason is the lower cost - a pound of bushmeat may sell for 20 US cents.

The problem of bushmeat making its way onto Kenyans' dinner plates is not new.

In 2004, a conservation group analyzed the meat from 202 butchers in Nairobi, finding that 25 percent of the products surveyed were bushmeat and 19 percent a mixture of game and meat from domestic animals.

A customer purchasing meat at the Burma Meat Market said the only safe meat is meat with a government stamp.

"We know that the shops we buy meat from is good, but there is some meat that is coming in paper bags, that meat when it comes we as customers buy it, there is no way for us to know if that meat is good or bad. However there is some other meat that you can see here it has a government stamp and we know that it is good because it has the stamp of approval from the Kenya Meat Commission," he said.

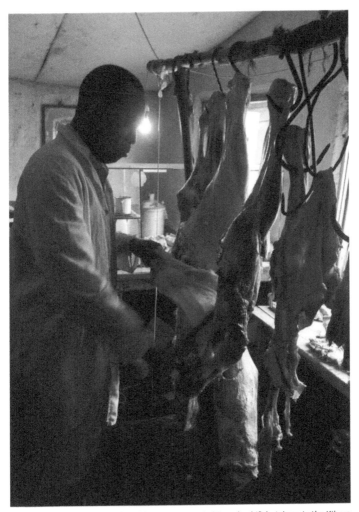

Peter Njoroge slices pieces of beef from a carcass, in his makeshift butchery in the Kibera slum in Nairobi, Kenya. According to Kenyan authorities, wild animals such as zebra and wildebeest that have been slaughtered illegally are frequently passed off as beef in the capital, prompting grave health concerns, July 10, 2007. (AP Photo/Khalil Senosi)

Slaughtering wildlife is illegal in Kenya.

The government banned sport hunting in 1977, but allowed limited hunting to cull animals and harvest game meat until 2003, when animal rights groups managed to shut it down.

## Bushmeat Traders in Ghana
Ghana
October 29, 2014
By The Associated Press

Yaa Kyerewaa waits for clients as she stands next to her makeshift bushmeat shop at one of the largest local markets in Accra, Ghana. This "bushmeat" was once considered a delicacy and fetched premium prices but Ebola has frightened away customers and it has been many days since Kyerewaa sold anything, so she cuts a sullen figure as she stands beside a pile of animal parts including the jaws of giant rodents, the hooves of wild pigs and snails, October 22, 2014. (AP Photo/Christian Thompson)

Yaa Kyerewaa cuts a lonely figure beside a pile of animal parts: the jaws of a giant rodent, the hooves of wild pigs, snails. This bushmeat was once considered a delicacy and fetched premium prices. But Ebola has frightened away customers and Kyerewaa hasn't sold anything in days.

Accra's busy Agbogbloshie market used to have several bushmeat vendors but now she is the only one.

The 53-year-old says her earnings from bush \meat keep her four children in school and she laments the sudden loss of business as public health officials warn that bushmeat may be contaminated with the dreaded Ebola virus.

"Bushmeat is healthy. I usually eat it as a special food on Sundays," she said. "We have been consuming for years only for it to be made unpopular by these needless rumors flying around. No one wants to buy our products now. It is sad."

Bushmeat is displayed for sale at one of the largest local markets in Accra, Ghana, October 22, 2014. (AP Photo/Christian Thompson)

Many restaurants in Ghana's capital no longer serve bushmeat, of which a large rodent known as a "grasscutter" was the most popular offering. Hunters trap them in the wild or rear them at home for their meat, which is said to taste like chicken.

Health experts believe the initial cases in many Ebola outbreaks start from people eating or handling Ebola-infected animals. Then they spread it to other people through contact with bodily fluids. Fruit bats, as well as primates such as chimpanzees, are frequently cited as potential reservoirs of the Ebola virus — animals many Africans hunt for their meat.

Human infections in Africa have been linked to hunting, butchering and processing meat from infected animals, although none from eating cooked bushmeat, according to the U.S. Centers for Disease Control and Prevention. Ebola first appeared in 1976 in Congo and has caused periodic outbreaks there and in other African countries. This is West Africa's first outbreak — and the most deadly ever — and the World Health Organization warns it could get worse before the situation improves. More than 4,500 people, mostly in Guinea, Sierra Leone and Liberia, have died.

While stemming human-to-human transmission is the main focus for governments and international health agencies, African communities that hunt wild animals for their meat "risk future spill-over from species that can carry the virus," including fruit bats, some primates, and small antelopes called duikers, the Food and Agriculture Organization warns. Hunting animals that are sick or behaving strangely, or collecting dead animals for sale, is risky, the U.N. agency says.

Despite the dangers, bushmeat is a source of protein for many West Africans, and for some it is a special treat. The soup of a roasted fruit bat, for example, is highly sought after.

Kyerewaa said she once had clients from all walks of life. That has changed with Ebola sweeping through West Africa and health officials stepping up campaigns to educate the public about how to avoid catching it.

"I am the only surviving bushmeat seller in this market," said Kyerewaa, who said she has been a bushmeat trader for years. "I can't stop coming because I have to look for ways to support myself and my family."

At her stall the parts of the great cane rat —smoked and salted for preservation — fetch as much as $30. That's out of reach for many in Ghana, where many live on less than $2 a day.

Rebecca Ackwonu, a Ghana Health Service Commission official, said it's hard to enforce any kind of bushmeat ban in a country where many people grew up on it.

"We have advised our people to suspend eating bushmeat in the meantime because of the risks," she said.

Some have heeded the call.

Theodor Semi, who operates a popular downtown restaurant called Semi's Place, said he won't serve bushmeat until all of West Africa is declared free of Ebola.

"It has affected business, of course," he said. "It has become slow because most Ghanaians like bushmeat, especially grasscutter."

# 3

# Ebola Part I – Quarantine

Health workers teach people about the Ebola virus and how to prevent infection, in Conakry, Guinea. On March 30, Ebola crossed the border into Liberia, where the health minister said two patients have tested positive for the deadly virus, March 31, 2014. (AP Photo/ Youssouf Bah, File)

### The Beginning
Guinea
March 23, 2014
By Boubacar Diallo

Samples from victims of a viral hemorrhagic fever that has killed more than 50 people in Guinea have tested positive for the Ebola virus, government officials said Sunday, marking the first time an outbreak among humans has been detected in this West African nation.

Government spokesman Damantang Albert Camara said the virus was found in tests conducted at a laboratory in Lyon, France.

A Health Ministry statement on Saturday said 80 cases including 59 deaths had been reported, most of them in three southern prefectures near Sierra Leone and Liberia. Three cases, including two deaths, were reported in Conakry, the capital, according to the statement.

A team including the health minister had been dispatched to the region, Camara said, and Doctors without Borders had set up an isolation unit in Gueckedou to try to stop the disease from spreading.

"In Guinea, a country with a weak medical infrastructure, an outbreak like this can be devastating," Dr. Mohamed Ag Ayoya, country representative for UNICEF, said in a statement Sunday noting that three children had died in the outbreak.

Previous Ebola outbreaks have been reported in Congo and Uganda, most recently in 2012. The only prior case of a human contracting the virus in West Africa came in 1994, when a scientist fell ill while responding to Ebola cases among chimpanzees in a national park in Ivory Coast, said Dr. Esther Sterk, tropical disease adviser for Doctors Without Borders. The scientist eventually recovered.

Sterk, who is coordinating the Doctors Without Borders response from Geneva, said the organization had confirmed 49 cases including 29 deaths. Samples from six victims had been linked to Ebola, she said, though it was "quite likely" the others also contracted the virus.

"We see that a lot of people that died, they were all linked, meaning they have been in contact with each other," she said. "That is very typical for Ebola outbreaks. We see that there is a transmission chain in families."

Officials have not been able to determine how Ebola was introduced, though that can result from contact with an infected animal like a bat or a monkey.

Among humans the disease is transmitted through bodily fluids.

Officials have also been unable to determine the subtype of Ebola, which would give them a better idea of the fatality rate, Sterk said. The fatality rate for Ebola can range from 25 to 90 percent.

Sterk said there were concerns the disease could spread to neighboring West African countries Sierra Leone and Liberia.

Saturday's Health Ministry statement said one of the positive cases had traveled to Liberia.

Liberian Health Minister Walter Gwenigale said officials had been sent to regions bordering Guinea to increase surveillance and to educate health workers about how to protect themselves from harmful contact with the virus.

"There's definitely a risk but it all depends on the movement of the people," Sterk said.

## Awaiting Death in Wards
Conakry, Guinea
April 3, 2014
By Boubacar Diallo

Medical personnel at the emergency entrance of a hospital wait to receive suspected Ebola virus patients in Conakry, Guinea. The Ebola virus that has killed scores of people in Guinea in 2014 is a new strain _ evidence that the disease did not spread there from outbreaks in some other African nations, scientists reported Wednesday, April 16, 2014 in the New England Journal of Medicine. "The source of the virus is still not known," but it was not imported from nearby countries, said Dr. Stephan Gunther of the Bernhard Nocht Institute for Tropical Medicine in Hamburg, Germany, March 29, 2014. (AP Photo/Youssouf Bah)

Bakari Soumaoro carried his sick friend all the way to the hospital on his back, not realizing that the man's fever and chills were caused by one of the deadliest diseases on Earth.

A week after his friend died, Soumaoro himself fell ill.

Hospital officials soon determined that both men had contracted Ebola, a disease causing severe bleeding that had never before struck this corner of

West Africa. The outbreak has killed more than 86 people in Guinea and Liberia, and it's not over.

Soumaoro, a driver for an aid group, Plan International, died soon after symptoms appeared. Before long, everyone who had visited him at the hospital was placed into an isolation ward set up by health workers here.

"Fortunately after the waiting period we all tested negative, thanks be to God," said Mamady Drame, the local director for Plan International in Macenta, 715 kilometers (445 miles) southeast of the capital, Conakry.

Ebola is so virulent that those who do test positive can only wait to die in a special ward where they are treated by medical personnel wearing protective suits and gear. The Zaire strain detected in Guinea kills up to 90 percent of its victims, and with no cure all that can be done is to make patients comfortable as their organs begin failing.

The West African nation of Guinea is among the poorest in the world, and is severely lacking in health care facilities outside Conakry. Those who have been exposed to Ebola in southern Guinea are kept in one ward. If it's confirmed they do have Ebola, they then are moved to the second pavilion to await death.

Three more suspected cases were put into quarantine on Wednesday in Macenta, where already 14 people have died.

It's a similar situation in neighboring Liberia, where health officials say the deaths of two sisters have been confirmed as Ebola. One of the women left behind a baby and a husband who are now in isolation.

The cases have been dramatic: One man dropped dead only 30 minutes after he arrived at a hospital in Liberia. Another person was taken not to a clinic, but to a church for a prayer of divine intervention. She died on Wednesday.

Amid Ebola's near-certain death sentence, fear and panic have spread. Passengers fled a bus after an elderly man vomited on board. In neighboring Liberia, one market emptied out when people falsely believed they could catch the disease simply from breathing the same air as victims. In Liberia's capital, Monrovia, cashiers at one grocery store wore rubber gloves to protect themselves.

In southern Guinea, church pews are now empty on Sundays. People are fearful of shaking hands and instead make the sign of the cross when they greet a friend or loved one.

"Here it's like time has stopped. Every day is potentially dangerous for us. And it's only God who can save us from this disease," said Lalla Balde, who lives in Macenta.

"We don't know what sin we have committed so that the Ebola fever has befallen us," said another resident, Cece Lohalamou. "We already have enough problems here."

## New Strain
### Washington
### April 16, 2014
### By Marilynn Marchione

A woman being discharged from the Island Clinic Ebola treatment center in Monrovia, Liberia, is sprayed with disinfectant, September 30, 2014. (AP Photo/Jerome Delay, File)

The Ebola virus that has killed scores of people in Guinea this year is a new strain — evidence that the disease did not spread there from outbreaks in some other African nations, scientists report.

"The source of the virus is still not known," but it was not imported from nearby countries, said Dr. Stephan Gunther of the Bernhard Nocht Institute for Tropical Medicine in Hamburg, Germany.

He led an international team of researchers who studied the genetics of the virus and reported results online Wednesday in the New England Journal of Medicine.

The ongoing outbreak has caused panic and killed more than 120 people in West Africa, mostly in Guinea, according to the World Health Organization.

Ebola (ee-BOH'-lah) causes internal bleeding and organ failure and is fatal in 30 percent to 90 percent of cases, depending on the strain. It spreads through direct contact with infected people, and some earlier cases have been linked to certain fruit bats that live in West Africa.

There is no cure or vaccine, so containing the outbreak has focused on supportive care for those infected with the virus and isolating them to limit its spread.

Earlier, health officials had said the Guinea Ebola was a Zaire strain, different from the kind that has caused cases in other parts of Africa. The Democratic Republic of Congo used to be called Zaire.

The new research analyzed blood samples from 20 patients in the current outbreak and found the strain was unique.

"It is not coming from the Democratic Republic of Congo. It has not been imported to Guinea" from that country or from Gabon, where Ebola also has occurred, Gunther said.

Researchers think the Guinea and other strains evolved in parallel from a recent ancestor virus. The Guinea outbreak likely began last December or earlier and might have been smoldering for some time unrecognized. The investigation continues to try to identify "the presumed animal source," they write.

### The Stigma of Survival
Conakry, Guinea
April 27, 2014
By Boubacar Ciallo and Sarah DiLorenzo

The doctor has beaten the odds and survived Ebola, but he still has one more problem: The stigma carried by the deadly disease.

Even though he is completely healthy, people are afraid to come near him or to have anything to do with him.

For example, the man was supposed to give an interview on Guinean radio to describe his triumphant tale. But the station would not allow him into the studio.

"We'd prefer he speak by phone from downstairs," the station's director told a representative of Doctors Without Borders, while the survivor waited outside in a car. "I can't take the risk of letting him enter our studio."

United Nations Secretary-General Ban Ki-moon speaks at a press conference in Addis Ababa, Ethiopia. Ban Ki-moon, speaking on a trip to Ethiopia on Monday, called health workers managing the Ebola outbreak in West Africa "exceptional people" and said the situation for returning health workers from Ebola-affected countries is proving difficult and that the stigma against them should end, October 27, 2014. (AP Photo)

The Ebola outbreak in West Africa has claimed more than 145 lives so far. More than 240 people, mostly in Guinea, are suspected of having caught the illness, which causes horrific suffering, including bursting blood vessels and bleeding from ears and other orifices. There is no vaccine, no treatment and the disease is almost always fatal.

But a handful of the infected do survive. About 30 patients have survived in Guinea so far, according to Doctors Without Borders. Liberia has not recorded any cases of survival.

Unfortunately for the lucky few, the stink of stigma lingers long after the virus has been purged from their bodies.

"Thanks be to God, I am cured. But now I have a new disease: the stigmatization that I am a victim of," said the Guinean doctor, who spoke to The Associated Press but refused to give his name for fear of further problems the publicity would cause him and his family. "This disease (the stigma) is worse than the fever."

Several other people who survived the disease refused to tell their stories when contacted by the AP, either directly or through Doctors Without Borders.

Sam Taylor, the Doctors Without Borders spokesman who had taken the doctor to the radio station, confirmed that the man had been infected and survived.

The doctor believes he caught Ebola while caring for a friend and colleague who died in Conakry, Guinea's capital. At the time, he said, he did not know that his friend had Ebola.

Shortly after his friend's death, the doctor got a headache and came down with an intractable fever. And then the vomiting and diarrhea began.

"I should have died," the doctor said, but he responded to care, which includes intensive hydration, and unlike most other Ebola patients, he lived.

Surviving Ebola is a matter of staying alive long enough to have the chance to develop enough antibodies to fight off the virus, said David Heymann, a professor of infectious disease epidemiology at the London School of Hygiene & Tropical Medicine.

That's because it's typically the symptoms of Ebola — severe fever, hemorrhaging, dehydration, respiratory problems — that kills a patient.

Even though he has been cleared of Ebola, the doctor says that people avoid him.

"Now, everywhere in my neighborhood, all the looks bore into me like I'm the plague," he said. People leave places when he shows up. No one will shake his hand or eat with him. His own brothers are accusing him of putting their family in danger.

Stigma often accompanies the spread of deadly, poorly understood diseases, said Meredith Stakem, a health and nutrition adviser for Catholic Relief Services in West Africa, noting that the terrified reaction to Ebola recalls the early days of the HIV epidemic.

Ebola may incite an even more severe reaction because health workers responding to it wear head-to-toe protective gear that look like space suits, Stakem noted.

In this outbreak, the homes of some of the infected in Liberia have been attacked and Doctors Without Borders briefly abandoned a clinic in Guinea that was targeted.

The families of those who die from Ebola face similar problems.

Aziz Soumah, who lives in a suburb of the Guinean capital of Conakry, said his family was forced to move after his brother died, apparently from Ebola.

"I went to pray at the mosque. As soon as I entered, all the worshippers left the mosque," recounted Soumah, a 30-year-old engineer. "I was alone. No one around me."

International health organizations are doing extensive community outreach to explain how the disease is transmitted — only through direct contact with the bodily fluids of symptomatic people — and to explain that those cured are no longer contagious.

The most powerful tool to combat stigma is the way health care workers treat a discharged patient, said Corinne Benazech, the representative in Guinea for Doctors Without Borders in Guinea.

"The patient never leaves alone," she said of when Ebola survivors leave their isolation wards, and health care workers individually shake hands with the survivor.

Discharged patients receive a certificate from the minister of health that states they are no longer contagious, said Tom Fletcher, an infectious disease physician with the World Health Organization who is working in Guinea. However, the virus may linger in a male patient's semen, so men are given a three-month supply of condoms, he added.

The Guinean doctor was treated for about a week before he was declared cured. Fletcher said that's typical for the miraculous few: "These people should be celebrated, really, as opposed to stigmatized."

### Arriving in Sierra Leon
Freetown, Sierra Leon
June 12, 2014
By Clarence Roy-Macaulay

The Sierra Leone government announced a state of emergency in the Kailahun district from the outbreak of the Ebola virus which has claimed 17 lives in this West African nation, banning public gatherings and closing schools.

According to government figures released Thursday, June 12, 2014 there are 46 confirmed cases and another 122 suspected ones in the district near the border with Liberia.

A healthcare worker in protective gear sprays disinfectant around the house of a person suspected to have Ebola virus in Port Loko Community, situated on the outskirts of Freetown, Sierra Leone, October 21, 2014. (AP Photo/Michael Duff)

In a press conference Wednesday, however, local parliamentarian Momoh Moiwai said the death toll was actually 28.

The government statement issued Wednesday night said all schools in the district will be closed to minimize Ebola transmission, while public gatherings including cinemas and night clubs would be prohibited.

Vehicles entering and leaving the district will also be screened at checkpoints, added the statement.

More than a month after Guinea President Alpha Conde told reporters the Ebola outbreak that originated in his country was under control, the death toll continues to climb in his country as well as in Sierra Leone and Liberia.

At least 231 people have died since the outbreak of the fearsome disease, which causes bleeding internally and externally and for which there is no known cure. Guinea, where the outbreak began, has recorded just over 200 deaths.

Experts say the outbreak may have begun as far back as January in southeast Guinea. Ebola typically begins in remote places and it can take several infections before the disease is identified, making a precise start date virtually impossible to pin down.

It's one of the worst outbreaks since the disease was first recorded in 1976 in simultaneous outbreaks in Sudan and Congo, according to Doctors Without Borders and may wind up being the worst outbreak ever.

# 4

# Ebola Part II – Out of Control

People suspected of having Ebola receive treatment in the Hastings area of Freetown, Sierra Leone. Some doctors in countries hit hardest by the deadly Ebola disease decline to operate on pregnant women for fear the virus could spread. Governments face calls from frightened citizens to bar travel to and from the afflicted region. Meanwhile, the stakes get higher as more people get sick, highlighting a tricky balance between protecting people and preserving their rights in a global crisis, October 15, 2014. (AP Photo/Michael Duff)

Second Wave
Dakar, Senegal
June 20, 2014
By Sarah DiLorenzo

The Ebola outbreak ravaging West Africa is "totally out of control," according to a senior official for Doctors Without Borders, who says the medical group is stretched to the limit in responding.

The outbreak has caused more deaths than any other of the disease, said another official with the medical charity. Ebola has been linked to more than 330 deaths in Guinea, Sierra Leone and Liberia, according to the World Health Organization.

International organizations and the governments involved need to send in more health experts and increase public education messages about how to stop the spread of the disease, Bart Janssens, the director of operations for the medical group in Brussels, told The Associated Press on Friday, June 20, 2014.

"The reality is clear that the epidemic is now in a second wave," Janssens said. "And, for me, it is totally out of control."

The Ebola virus, which causes internal bleeding and organ failure, spreads through direct contact with infected people. There is no cure or vaccine, so containing an outbreak focuses on supportive care for the ill and isolating them to limit the spread of the virus.

The current outbreak, which began in Guinea either late last year or early this year, had appeared to slow before picking up pace again in recent weeks, including spreading to the Liberian capital for the first time.

"This is the highest outbreak on record and has the highest number of deaths, so this is unprecedented so far," said Armand Sprecher, a public health specialist with Doctors Without Borders.

According to the WHO, the highest previous death toll was in the first recorded Ebola outbreak in Congo in 1976, when 280 deaths were reported. Because Ebola often touches remote areas and the first cases sometimes go unrecognized, it is likely that there are deaths that go uncounted during outbreaks.

The multiple locations of the current outbreak and its movement across borders make it one of the "most challenging Ebola outbreaks ever," Fadela Chaib, a spokeswoman for the World Health Organization, said earlier in the week.

But Janssens' description of the Ebola outbreak was even more alarming, and he warned that the countries involved had not recognized the gravity of the situation. He criticized WHO for not doing enough to prod local leaders; the U.N. health agency did not immediately respond to requests for comment.

"There needs to be a real political commitment that this is a very big emergency," he said. "Otherwise, it will continue to spread, and for sure it will spread to more countries."

But Tolbert Nyenswah, Liberia's deputy minister of health, said the highest levels of government are working to contain the outbreak, noting that Liberia had a long period with no new cases before this second wave.

Governments and international agencies are definitely struggling to keep up with the outbreak, said Unni Krishnan of Plan International, which is providing equipment to the three countries. But he noted that the disease is striking in one of the world's poorest regions, where public health systems are already fragile.

With more than 40 international staff currently on the ground and four treatment centers, Doctors Without Borders has reached its limit to respond, Janssens said. It is unclear, for instance, if the group will be able to set up a treatment center in Liberia, like the ones it is running in in Guinea and Sierra Leone, he said.

Janssens said the only way to stop the disease's spread is to persuade people to come forward when symptoms occur and to avoid touching the sick and dead.

He said this outbreak is particularly challenging because it began in an area where people are very mobile and has spread to even more densely populated areas, like the capitals of Guinea and Liberia. The disease typically strikes sparsely populated areas in central or eastern Africa, where it spreads less easily, he said.

By contrast, the epicenter of this outbreak is near a major regional transport hub, the Guinean city of Gueckedou.

## 500 Plus
### Guinea
### July 14, 2014
### By Boubacr Diallo

Deep in the forests of southern Guinea, the first victims fell ill with high fevers. People assumed it was the perennial killer malaria and had no reason to fear touching the bodies, as is the custom in traditional funerals.

Some desperate relatives brought their loved ones to the distant capital in search of better medical care, unknowingly spreading what ultimately was discovered to be Ebola, one of the world's most deadly diseases.

Ebola, a hemorrhagic fever that can cause its victims to bleed from the ears and nose, had never before been seen in this part of West Africa where medical clinics are few and far between. The disease has turned up in at least two other countries — Liberia and Sierra Leone — and 539 deaths have been attributed to the outbreak that is now the largest on record.

Guinea Police secure the area around a man who collapsed in a puddle of water on the street, and people would not approach him as they fear he may be suffering from the Ebola virus in the city of Conakry, Guinea, August 6, 2014. (AP Photo/ Youssouf Bah)

The key to halting Ebola is isolating the sick, but fear and panic have sent some patients into hiding, complicating efforts to stop its spread. Ebola has reached the capitals of all three countries, and the World Health Organization reported 44 new cases including 21 deaths on Friday.

There has been "a gross misjudgment across the board in gauging the severity and scale of damage the current Ebola outbreak can unleash," the aid group Plan International warned earlier this month.

"There are no cases from outside Africa to date. The threat of it spreading though is very much there," said Dr. Unni Krishnan, head of disaster preparedness and response for the aid group.

Preachers are calling for divine intervention, and panicked residents in remote areas have on multiple occasions attacked the very health workers sent to help them. In one town in Sierra Leone, residents partially burned down a treatment center over fears that the drugs given to victims were actually causing the disease.

Activists are trying to spread awareness in the countryside where literacy is low, even through a song penned about Ebola.

"It has no cure, but it can be prevented; let us fight it together. Let's protect ourselves, our families and our nation," sings the chorus.

"Do not touch people with the signs of Ebola," sings musician and activist Juli Endee. "Don't eat bushmeat. Don't play with monkey and baboons. Plums that bats have bitten or half-eaten, don't eat them."

Guinea first notified WHO about the emergence of Ebola in March and soon after cases were reported in neighboring Liberia. Two months later there were hopes that the outbreak was waning, but then people began falling ill in Sierra Leone.

Doctors Without Borders says it fears the number of patients now being treated in Sierra Leone could be "just the tip of the iceberg." Nearly 40 were reported in a single village in the country's east.

"We're under massive time pressure: The longer it takes to find and follow up with people who have come in contact with sick people, the more difficult it will be to control the outbreak," said Anja Wolz, emergency coordinator for the group, also referred to by its French name Medecins Sans Frontieres.

This Ebola virus is a new strain and did not spread to West Africa from previous outbreaks in Uganda and Congo, researchers say. Many believe it is linked to the human consumption of bats carrying the virus. Many of those who have fallen ill in the current outbreak are family members of victims and the health workers who treated them.

There is no cure and no vaccine for Ebola, and those who have survived managed to do so only by receiving rehydration and other supportive treatment. Ebola's high fatality rate means many of those brought to health clinics have been merely kept as comfortable as possible in quarantine as they await death. As a result, some families have been afraid to take sick loved ones to the clinics.

"Let this warning go out: Anyone found or reported to be holding suspected Ebola cases in homes or prayer houses can be prosecuted under the law of Liberia," President Ellen Johnson Sirleaf stated recently.

Her comments came just days after Sierra Leone issued a similar warning, saying some patients had discharged themselves from the hospital and had gone into hiding.

At the airport in Guinea's capital, departing passengers must undergo temperature screening, and those with a fever are pulled aside for further evaluation. Still, the stigma of Ebola follows Guineans well outside the region.

"The police treated us like we were aliens. They said they didn't want us in their country because of the disease affecting Guinea," says Tafsir Sow, a businessman who was briefly detained at the airport in Casablanca, Morocco before continuing on to Paris. "I had tears in my eyes."

Still, WHO health officials are hopeful they will be able to get the situation under control in the next several weeks. A recent conference in the capital of Ghana brought together health authorities from across the affected areas, and the countries agreed on a common approach to fight Ebola.

"When you have it spread, of course it's moving in the wrong direction," said Dr. Keiji Fukuda, WHO's assistant director-general for health security and environment. "You want to see the number of infections going down. So we really have to redouble our efforts. But saying that it's out of control makes it sound like there are no solutions. This is a virus for which there are very clear solutions."

### Airborne Death
Abuja, Nigeria
July 26, 2014
By The Associated Press

A man reads a newspaper on a Lagos street with the headline Ebola Virus kills Liberian in Lagos. An Ebola outbreak that has left more than 660 people dead across West Africa has spread to the continent's most populous nation after a Liberian man with a high fever vomited aboard an airplane to Nigeria and then died there, officials said Friday. The 40-year-old man had recently lost his sister to Ebola in Liberia, health officials there said. It was not immediately clear how he managed to board a flight, but he was moved into an isolation ward upon arrival in Nigeria on Tuesday and died on Friday, the 25th, July 26, 2014. (AP Photo/Sunday Alamba)

Guinea Police secure the area in front of a man who collapsed in a puddle of water on the street. The man lay in the street for several hours before being taken to an Ebola control centre for assessment. The World Health Organization has began an emergency meeting on the Ebola crisis, and said at least 932 deaths in four countries are blamed on the virus, with many hundreds more being treated in quarantine conditions, August 6, 2014. (AP Photo/ Youssouf Bah)

Nigerian health authorities raced to stop the spread of Ebola on Saturday, July 26, 2014 after a man sick with one of the world's deadliest diseases brought it by plane to Lagos, Africa's largest city with 21 million people.

The fact that the traveler from Liberia could board an international flight also raised new fears that other passengers could take the disease beyond

Africa due to weak inspection of passengers and the fact Ebola's symptoms are similar to other diseases.

Officials in the country of Togo, where the sick man's flight had a stopover, also went on high alert after learning that Ebola could possibly have spread to a fifth country.

Screening people as they enter the country may help slow the spread of the disease, but it is no guarantee Ebola won't travel by airplane, according to Dr. Lance Plyler, who heads Ebola medical efforts in Liberia for aid organization Samaritan's Purse.

"Unfortunately the initial signs of Ebola imitate other diseases, like malaria or typhoid," he said.

The aid organization on Saturday said a U.S. doctor working with Ebola patients in Liberia had tested positive for the deadly virus. A Samaritan's Purse news release said Dr. Kent Brantly was being treated at a hospital in Monrovia, the capital.

Ebola already had caused some 672 deaths across a wide swath of West Africa before the Nigeria case was announced. It is the deadliest outbreak on record for Ebola, and now it threatens Nigeria, Africa's most populous nation. An outbreak in Lagos, Africa's megacity where many live in cramped conditions, could be a major disaster.

"Lagos is completely different from other cities because we're talking about millions of people," said Plan International's Disaster Response and Preparedness Head, Dr. Unni Krishnan.

Nigerian newspapers describe the effort as a "scramble" to contain the threat after the Liberian arrived in Lagos and then died Friday.

International airports in Nigeria are screening passengers arriving from foreign countries for symptoms of Ebola, according to Yakubu Dati, the spokesman for Federal Aviation Authority of Nigeria.

Health officials are also working with ports and land borders, he said. "They are giving out information in terms of enlightenment, what to do, what to look out for."

And Nigerian airports are setting up holding rooms to ready in case another potential Ebola victim lands in Nigeria.

Airports in Guinea, Liberia and Sierra Leone, the three other West African countries affected by the current Ebola outbreak, have implemented some preventive measures, according to officials in those countries. But none of the safeguards are foolproof, say health experts.

Doctors say health screens could be effective, but Ebola has a variable incubation period of between two and 21 days and cannot be diagnosed on the spot.

Patrick Sawyer, a consultant for the Liberian Ministry of Finance arrived in Nigeria on Tuesday and was immediately detained by health authorities suspecting he might have Ebola, Plyler said.

On his way to Lagos, Sawyer's plane also stopped in Lome, Togo, according to the World Health Organization.

Authorities announced Friday that blood tests from the Lagos University Teaching Hospital confirmed Sawyer died of Ebola earlier that day.

Sawyer reportedly did not show Ebola symptoms when he boarded the plane, Plyler said, but by the time he arrived in Nigeria he was vomiting and had diarrhea. There has not been another recently recorded case of Ebola spreading through air travel, he added.

Nearly 50 other passengers on the flight are being monitored for signs of Ebola but are not being kept in isolation, said an employee at Nigeria's Ministry of Health, who insisted on anonymity because he was not authorized to speak to the press.

Sawyer's sister also died of Ebola in Liberia, according to Liberian officials, but he claimed to have had no contact with her. Ebola is highly contagious and kills more than 70 percent of people infected.

Ebola is passed by touching bodily fluids of patients even after they die, he said. Traditional burials that include rubbing the bodies of the dead contribute to the spread of the disease, Krishnan added.

There is no "magic bullet" cure for Ebola, but early detection and treatment of fluids and nutrition can be effective, said Plyler in Liberia. Quickly isolating patients who show symptoms is also crucial in slowing the spread of the disease.

West African hospital systems have weak and "often paralyzed" health care systems, he added, and are not usually equipped to handle Ebola outbreaks. International aid organizations like his and Doctors Without Borders have stepped in, but they also lack enough funding and manpower. "We need more humanitarian workers," he said. "We need resources."

## New Fear
Dakar, Senegal
July 28, 2014
By Krista Larson and Maria Cheng

Women walk past the entrance to the University Hospital Fann, where a man is being treated for symptoms of the Ebola virus in Dakar, Senegal. A man infected with Ebola traveled to Senegal, becoming the first recorded in this country of an outbreak that has hit four other West African countries and has killed more than 1,500 people, the Ministry of Health said Friday, August 29, 2014. (AP Photo/Jane Hahn)

No one knows for sure just how many people Patrick Sawyer came into contact with the day he boarded a flight in Liberia, had a stopover in Ghana, changed planes in Togo, and then arrived in Nigeria, where authorities say he died days later from Ebola, one of the deadliest diseases known to man.

Now health workers are scrambling to trace those who may have been exposed to Sawyer across West Africa, including flight attendants and fellow passengers.

Health experts say it is unlikely he could have infected others with the virus that can cause victims to bleed from the eyes, mouth and ears. Still, unsettling questions remain: How could a man whose sister recently died from Ebola manage to board a plane leaving the country? And worse: Could Ebola become the latest disease to be spread by international air travel?

Sawyer's death on Friday, July 25, 2014 has led to tighter screening of airline passengers in West Africa, where an unprecedented outbreak that emerged in March has killed more than 670 people in Guinea, Sierra Leone and Liberia. But some health authorities expressed little confidence in such precautions.

"The best thing would be if people did not travel when they were sick, but the problem is people won't say when they're sick. They will lie in order to travel, so it is doubtful travel recommendations would have a big impact," said Dr. David Heymann, professor of infectious diseases at the London School of Hygiene and Tropical Medicine.

"The important thing is for countries to be prepared when they get patients infected with Ebola, that they are isolated, family members are told what to do and health workers take the right steps."

The World Health Organization is awaiting laboratory confirmation after Nigerian health authorities said Sawyer tested positive for Ebola, WHO spokesman Gregory Hartl said. The WHO has not recommended any travel restrictions since the outbreak came to light.

"We would have to consider any travel recommendations very carefully, but the best way to stop this outbreak is to put the necessary measures in place at the source of infection," Hartl said. Closing borders "might help, but it won't be exhaustive or foolproof."

The risk of travelers contracting Ebola is considered low because it requires direct contact with bodily fluids or secretions such as urine, blood, sweat or saliva, experts say. Ebola can't be spread like flu through casual contact or breathing in the same air.

Patients are contagious only once the disease has progressed to the point they show symptoms, according to the WHO. And the most vulnerable are health care workers and relatives who come in much closer contact with the sick.

Still, witnesses say Sawyer, a 40-year-old Liberian Finance Ministry employee en route to a conference in Nigeria, was vomiting and had diarrhea aboard at least one of his flights with some 50 other passengers aboard. Ebola can be contracted from traces of feces or vomit, experts say.

Sawyer was immediately quarantined upon arrival in Lagos — a city of 21 million people — and Nigerian authorities say his fellow travelers were advised of Ebola's symptoms and then were allowed to leave. The incubation period can be as long as 21 days, meaning anyone infected may not fall ill for several weeks.

Health officials rely on "contact tracing" — locating anyone who may have been exposed, and then anyone who may have come into contact with that person. That may prove impossible, given that other passengers journeyed on to dozens of other cities.

Patrick Sawyer had planned to visit his family in Minnesota next month to attend two of his three daughters' birthdays, his wife, Decontee Sawyer, told KSTP-TV in Minnesota.

"It's a global problem because Patrick could have easily come home with Ebola, easy," she said. The Associated Press left phone and email messages for her Monday.

International travel has made the spread of disease via airplanes almost routine. Outbreaks of measles, polio and cholera have been traced back to countries thousands of miles away. Even Ebola previously traveled the globe this way: During an outbreak in Ivory Coast in the 1990s, the virus infected a veterinarian who traveled to Switzerland, where the disease was snuffed out upon arrival and she ultimately survived, experts say.

Two American aid workers in Liberia have tested positive for the virus and are being treated there. U.S. health officials said Monday that the risk of the deadly germ spreading to the United States is remote.

The mere prospect of Ebola in Africa's most populous nation has Nigerians on edge.

In Nigeria's capital, Abuja, Alex Akinwale, a 35-year-old entrepreneur, said he is particularly concerned about taking the bus, which is the only affordable way to travel.

"It's actually making me very nervous. If I had my own car, I would be safer," he said. "The doctors are on strike, and that means they are not prepared for it. For now I'm trying to be very careful."

It's an unprecedented public health scenario: Since 1976, when the virus was first discovered, Ebola outbreaks were limited to remote corners of Congo and Uganda, far from urban centers, and stayed within the borders of a single country. This time, cases first emerged in Guinea, and before long hundreds of others were stricken in Liberia and Sierra Leone.

Those are some of the poorest countries in the world, with few doctors and nurses to treat sick patients let alone determine who is well enough to travel. In Sawyer's case, it appears nothing was done to question him until he fell sick on his second flight with Asky Airlines. An airline spokesman would not comment on what precautions were being taken in the aftermath of Sawyer's journey.

Liberian Assistant Health Minister Tolbert Nyenswah told The Associated Press last week that there had been no screening at Liberia's Monrovia airport. That changed quickly over the weekend, when President Ellen Johnson Sirleaf said a new policy on inspecting and testing all outgoing and incoming passengers will be strictly observed. She also announced that some borders were being closed and communities with large numbers of Ebola cases would be quarantined.

International travelers departing from the capitals of Sierra Leone and Guinea are also being checked for signs of fever, airport officials said. Buckets of chlorine are also on hand at Sierra Leone's airport in Freetown for disinfection, authorities said.

Still, detecting Ebola in departing passengers might be tricky, since its initial symptoms are similar to many other diseases, including malaria and typhoid fever.

"It will be very difficult now to contain this outbreak because it's spread," Heymann said. "The chance to stop it quickly was months ago before it crossed borders ... but this can still be stopped if there is good hospital infection control, contact tracing and collaboration between countries."

Nigerian authorities so far have identified 59 people who came into contact with Sawyer and have tested 20, said Lagos State Health Commissioner Jide Idris. Among them were officials from ECOWAS, a West African governing body, airline employees, health workers and the Nigerian ambassador to Liberia, he said. He said there have been no new cases of the disease.

The death toll from the worst recorded Ebola outbreak in history surpassed 700 in West Africa as security forces went house-to-house in Sierra Leone's capital Thursday, July 31, 2014, looking for patients and others exposed to the disease.

Fears grew as the United States warned against travel to the three infected countries — Guinea, Sierra Leone and Liberia — and Sierra Leone's soccer team was blocked from boarding a plane in Nairobi, Kenya, that was to take them to the Seychelles for a game on Saturday. Airport authorities in Kenya said Seychelles immigration told them to prevent the team from traveling.

Almost half of the 57 new deaths reported by the World Health Organization occurred in Liberia, where two Americans, Dr. Kent Brantly of Texas and Nancy Writebol, a North Carolina-based missionary, are also sick with Ebola.

## 700 and Counting
Freetown, Sierra Leon
July 31, 2014
By The Associated Press

A man washes his hands with disinfectant to prevent Ebola infection before entering a hospital in the capital city of Freetown, Sierra Leone. Ebola, a hemorrhagic fever that can cause its victims to bleed from the ears and nose, had never before been seen in this part of West Africa where medical clinics are few and far between, July 15, 2014. (AP Photo/Youssouf Bah)

At the White House, press secretary Josh Earnest said the U.S. is looking into options to bring them back to the U.S. Officials at Atlanta's Emory University Hospital said they expected one of the Americans to be transferred there "within the next several days." The hospital declined to identify which aid worker, citing privacy laws.

Writebol is in stable but serious condition and is receiving an experimental treatment that doctors hope will better address her condition, according to a statement released by SIM, a Christian missions organization. Her husband, David, is close by but can only visit his wife through a window or dressed in a haz-mat suit, the statement said.

"There was only enough (of the experimental serum) for one person. Dr. Brantly asked that it be given to Nancy Writebol," said Franklin Graham, president of Samaritan's Purse, another aid organization that has been working in Liberia during the Ebola crisis.

Brantly, who works for the aid group, did receive a unit of blood from a 14-year-old boy who had survived Ebola because of the doctor's care, Graham said in a statement.

"The young boy and his family wanted to be able to help the doctor who saved his life," he said.

Giving a survivor's blood to a patient might be aimed at seeing whether any antibodies the survivor made to the virus could help someone else fight off the infection. This approach has been tried in previous Ebola outbreaks with mixed results.

No further details were provided on the experimental treatment. There is currently no licensed drug or vaccine for Ebola, and patients can only be given supportive care to keep them hydrated. There are a handful of experimental drug and vaccine candidates for Ebola and while some have had promising results in animals including monkeys, none has been rigorously tested in humans.

The disease has continued to spread through bodily fluids as sick people remain out in the community and cared for by relatives without protective gear. People have become ill from touching sick family members and in some cases from soiled linens.

In Sierra Leone, which borders Liberia to the northwest, authorities are vowing to quarantine all those at home who have refused to go to isolation centers. Many families have kept relatives at home to pray for their survival instead of bringing them to clinics that have had a 60 percent fatality rate. Those in the throngs of death can bleed from their eyes, mouth and ears.

Rosa Crestani, Ebola emergency coordinator for Doctors Without Borders, also known as Medecins Sans Frontieres, said it is "crucial" at this point to gain the trust of communities that have been afraid to let health workers in and to deploy more medical staff.

"The declaration of a state of emergency in Sierra Leone shows a recognition of the gravity of the situation, but we do not yet know what this will mean on the ground. What we can say is that it will be difficult to implement due to the fact that the cases are dispersed over such a large area, and that we currently do not have a clear picture of where all the hotspots are," she said.

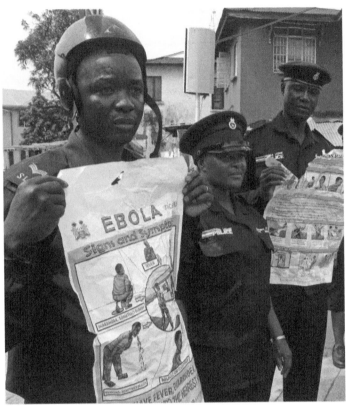

Sierra Leone police officers hold up posters as they try to educate people about the deadly Ebola virus in the city of Freetown, Sierra Leone. The global Ebola outbreak touched American shores more definitively Monday, as Atlanta awaited the arrival of its second Ebola patient by morning, and a New York hospital announced it had isolated a man with possible symptoms who walked into its emergency room, August 4, 2014. (AP Photo/ Youssouf Bah)

Liberia's president on Wednesday, the 30th, also instituted new measures aimed at halting the spread of Ebola, including shutting down schools and ordering most public servants to stay home from work.

"It could be helpful for the government to have powers to isolate and quarantine people and it's certainly better than what's been done so far," said Dr. Heinz Feldmann, chief of virology at U.S. National Institute of Allergy and Infectious Diseases. "Whether it works, we will have to wait and see."

Dr. Unni Krishnan, head of disaster preparedness and response for the aid group Plan International, said closing schools could help as they bring large numbers of children together, which can amplify infection rates.

"Door-to-door searches are not going to be easy," he said. "What will help is encouraging people to come forward when they see symptoms and seek medical help."

The U.S. Peace Corps also was evacuating hundreds of its volunteers in the affected countries. Two Peace Corps workers are under isolation outside the U.S. after having contact with a person who later died from the Ebola virus, a State Department official said.

In Moberly, Missouri, Liz Sosniecki said she got a call from her 25-year-old son, Dane, a Peace Corps volunteer in Liberia. He had not been exposed to Ebola and expressed disappointment about leaving just six weeks after he arrived.

"He said, 'I'm coming home.' Sorry," she said, beginning to cry. "I'm a little emotional. It's a relief."

The last time the U.S. Centers for Disease Control and Prevention issued such a travel warning during a disease outbreak was in 2003 because of SARS in Asia.

Ebola now has been blamed for 729 deaths in four West African countries this year: 339 in Guinea, 233 in Sierra Leone, 156 in Liberia and one in Nigeria.

The World Health Organization is launching a $100 million response plan calling for the deployment of several hundred additional health workers to help the strained resources in deeply impoverished West Africa, where hospital and clinics are ill-equipped to cope with routine health threats let alone the outbreak of a virulent disease like Ebola.

Among the deaths announced this week was that of the chief doctor treating Ebola in Sierra Leone, who was buried Thursday. The government said Dr. Sheik Humarr Khan's death was "an irreparable loss of this son of the soil." The 39-year-old was a leading doctor on hemorrhagic fevers in a nation with very few medical resources.

The Ebola cases first emerged in Guinea back in March, and later spread across the borders to Liberia and Sierra Leone. Outbreaks of the virus in previous years had occurred in other parts of Africa.

The current outbreak is now the largest recorded in world history, and has infected three African capitals with international airports. Officials are trying to step up screening of passengers, though an American man was able to fly from Liberia to Nigeria, where authorities say he died days later from Ebola.

Experts say the risk of travelers contracting it is considered low because it requires direct contact with bodily fluids or secretions such as urine, blood, sweat or saliva. Ebola can't be spread like flu through casual contact or breathing in the same air.

Patients are contagious only once the disease has progressed to the point they show symptoms, according to the World Health Organization. The most vulnerable are health care workers and relatives who come in much closer contact with the sick.

In Liberia, authorities say 28 out of the 45 health workers who have contracted the disease so far have died.

# 5

# Ebola Part III – Containment?

A health worker sprays the hands of a man with chlorinated water, before he enters a building as part of an Ebola prevention campaign in the city of Freetown, Sierra Leone, August 6, 2014. (AP Photo/ Michael Duff)

Treatment
London
August 1, 2014
By Maria Cheng

In the four decades since the Ebola virus was first identified in Africa, treatment hasn't changed much. There are no licensed drugs or vaccines for the deadly disease.

Some are being developed, but none have been rigorously tested in humans. One experimental treatment, though, was tried this week in an American aid worker sick with Ebola, according to the U.S-based group that she works for in Liberia.

Without a specific treatment, doctors and nurses focus on easing the disease's symptoms — fever, headache, vomiting and diarrhea — and on keeping patients hydrated and comfortable.

The outbreak in three West African countries — Liberia, Guinea and Sierra Leone — has sickened more than 1,300 people and more than 700 have died since March.

## WHY ISN'T THERE A TREATMENT BY NOW?

For one thing, the Ebola virus is hard to work with. The virus doesn't grow well in petri dishes and experiments can only be done in the relatively few labs with the highest security measures.

And while Ebola is lethal, it's rare. Outbreaks are unpredictable, giving doctors few chances to test new treatments. While the current epidemic is the largest recorded, the number of people sickened by Ebola is small compared to the number killed by other diseases like malaria or dengue. Much of the funding for Ebola research is from governments that worry about the virus being used in a bioterror attack.

"It's not economically viable for any company to do this kind of research because they have stockholders to think about," said Ben Neuman, a virologist at the University of Reading in Britain.

## WHAT'S IN THE PIPELINE?

There are about a half dozen Ebola drugs and vaccines in development, several of which have received funding from the U.S. One drug developed by the U.S. Army has shown promising results when tested in monkeys.

"We think this may work because of the animal models but until you do the studies in humans, you just don't know," said Fred Hayden, an infectious diseases specialist at the University of Virginia, who was not involved in the research.

While animal studies for vaccine candidates have been encouraging, it's unclear what dose humans would need.

A Canadian company, Tekmira, has a $140 million contract with the U.S. government to develop a Ebola vaccine. An early test of the shot in healthy humans was stopped recently after the Food and Drug Administration asked for more safety information.

A public information board explains the symptoms of the deadly Ebola virus in the city of Freetown, Sierra Leone. The global Ebola outbreak touched American shores more definitively Monday, as Atlanta awaited the arrival of its second Ebola patient by morning, and a New York hospital announced it had isolated a man with possible symptoms who walked into its emergency room, August 4, 2014. (AP Photo/ Youssouf Bah)

## SHOULD EXPERIMENTAL DRUGS BE USED NOW?

Scientists are split on whether or not it is a good idea to try experimental drugs and vaccines before they are approved but the prospect is being informally discussed.

"Given the prolonged and unprecedented nature of the epidemic, we need to carefully consider this," said Dr. Peter Piot, the co-discoverer of Ebola in 1976 and director of the London School of Hygiene and Tropical Medicine.

The World Health Organization has no plans to facilitate any clinical trials during this outbreak, spokesman Gregory Hartl said.

Other experts say it's unethical to use treatments or vaccines that haven't been properly tested, and warn the results could be disastrous.

"None of these drugs or vaccines are ready to be used in humans from a legal point of view," said Dr. Heinz Feldmann, chief of virology at the U.S. National Institute of Allergy and Infectious Diseases.

It would be impossible to vaccinate or treat everyone in the region but if any tests do proceed, they would probably be focused on those at highest risk: health care workers.

The American woman who got the experimental drug in Liberia worked at a hospital where Ebola patients were treated. It's not known what kind of treatment she received.

If health care workers are treated, "We will have to explain why some people are getting the vaccine and others are not," Feldmann said, adding there are still vast areas of West African communities suspicious of Western aid workers and their treatments. "At the moment, it doesn't even look like the local population wants it."

## Ebola in the U.S.
### Atlanta
### August 2, 2014
### By Ray Henry

The first Ebola victim to be brought to the United States from Africa was safely escorted into a specialized isolation unit Saturday, August 2, 2014 at one of the nation's best hospitals, where doctors said they are confident the deadly virus won't escape.

Fear that the outbreak killing more than 700 people in Africa could spread in the U.S. has generated considerable anxiety among some Americans. But infectious disease experts said the public faces zero risk as Emory University Hospital treats a critically ill missionary doctor and a charity worker who were infected in Liberia.

The U.S. Centers for Disease Control and Prevention has received "nasty emails" and at least 100 calls from people saying "How dare you bring Ebola into the country!?" CDC Director Dr. Tom Frieden told The Associated Press Saturday.

"I hope that our understandable fear of the unfamiliar does not trump our compassion when ill Americans return to the U.S. for care," Frieden said.

Dr. Kent Brantly and Nancy Writebol, who will arrive in several days, will be treated in Emory's isolation unit for infectious diseases, created 12 years ago to handle doctors who get sick at the CDC, just up the hill. It is one of about four in the country, equipped with everything necessary to test and treat people exposed to very dangerous viruses.

In 2005, it handled patients with SARS, which unlike Ebola can spread when an infected person coughs or sneezes.

In fact, the nature of Ebola — which is spread by close contact with bodily fluids and blood — means that any modern hospital using standard, rigorous, infection-control measures should be able to handle it.

Still, Emory won't be taking any chances.

"Nothing comes out of this unit until it is non-infectious," said Dr. Bruce Ribner, who will be treating the patients. "The bottom line is: We have an inordinate amount of safety associated with the care of this patient. And we do not believe that any health care worker, any other patient or any visitor to our facility is in any way at risk of acquiring this infection."

Brantly was flown from Africa to Dobbins Air Reserve base outside Atlanta in a small plane equipped to contain infectious diseases, and a small police escort followed his ambulance to the hospital. He climbed out dressed head to toe in white protective clothing, and another person in an identical hazardous materials suit held both of his gloved hands as they walked gingerly inside.

"It was a relief to welcome Kent home today. I spoke with him, and he is glad to be back in the U.S.," said his wife, Amber Brantly, who left Africa with their two young children for a wedding in the U.S. days before the doctor fell ill.

"I am thankful to God for his safe transport and for giving him the strength to walk into the hospital," her statement said.

Inside the unit, patients are sealed off from anyone who doesn't wear protective gear.

"Negative air pressure" means air flows in, but can't escape until filters scrub any germs from patients. All laboratory testing is conducted within the unit, and workers are highly trained in infection control. Glass walls enable staff outside to safely observe patients, and there's a vestibule where workers suit up before entering. Any gear is safely disposed of or decontaminated.

Family members will be kept outside for now.

The unit "has a plate glass window and communication system, so they'll be as close as 1-2 inches from each other," Ribner said.

Dr. Jay Varkey, an infectious disease specialist who will be treating Brantly and Writebol, gave no word Saturday about their condition. Both were described as critically ill after treating Ebola patients at a missionary hospital in Liberia, one of four West African countries hit by the largest outbreak of the virus in history.

There is no proven cure for the virus. It kills an estimated 60 percent to 80 percent of the people it infects, but American doctors in Africa say the mortality rate would be much lower in a functioning health care system.

The virus causes hemorrhagic fever, headaches and weakness that can escalate to vomiting, diarrhea and kidney and liver problems. Some patients bleed internally and externally.

There are experimental treatments, but Brantly had only enough for one person, and insisted that his colleague receive it. His best hope in Africa was the transfusion of blood he received including antibodies from one of his patients, a 14-year-old boy who survived thanks to the doctor.

There was also only room on the plane for one patient at a time. Writebol will follow in several days.

Dr. Philip Brachman, an Emory public health specialist who led the CDC's disease detectives program for many years, said Friday that since there is no cure, medical workers will try any modern therapy that can be done, such as better monitoring of fluids, electrolytes and vital signs.

"We depend on the body's defenses to control the virus," Dr. Ribner said. "We just have to keep the patient alive long enough in order for the body to control this infection."

Just down the street from the hospital, people dined, shopped and carried on with their lives Saturday. Several interviewed by the AP said the patients are coming to the right place.

"We've got the best facilities in the world to deal with this stuff," said Kevin Whalen, who lives in Decatur, Ga., and has no connection to Emory or the CDC. "With the resources we can throw at it, it's the best chance this guy has for survival. And it's probably also the best chance to develop treatments and cures and stuff that we can take back overseas so that it doesn't come back here."

A second American missionary stricken with Ebola returned to the U.S. for treatment, following a colleague who was admitted over the first weekend of August to Emory University Hospital's infectious disease unit.

## U.S. Missionary
### Atlanta
August 4, 2014
By Bill Barrow and Krista Larson

A child waits with other stranded people as they stand at a roadblock waiting to cross into Sierra Leone on the border that separates Guinea and Sierra Leone, and works as a makeshift border control checkpoint at Gbalamuya-Pamelap, Guinea. As Guinea closed its border with Sierra Leone at the weekend in an attempt to halt the spread of the deadly Ebola virus, people and goods were not able to cross to either side, August 12, 2014. (AP Photo/ Youssouf Bah)

Nancy Writebol departed with a medical evacuation team. The official, Information Minister Lewis Brown, said the evacuation flight left West Africa between 1 a.m. and 1.30 a.m. local time Tuesday, August 5, 2014.

Writebol's son, Jeremy Writebol of Wichita, Kansas, said his mother "is still struggling" but that "there seems to be improvement" and that the family is optimistic she will recover amid a spreading Ebola outbreak that has killed at least 729 people in Liberia, Guinea and Sierra Leone.

The Writebols' mission team partner, Dr. Kent Brantly, also was improving Sunday after he was admitted to Emory's quarantine unit a day earlier, according to a statement from his wife.

Nancy Writebol, who spent weeks in isolation after contracting the deadly Ebola virus in Liberia, holds a news conference in Charlotte, N.C. with her husband, David. This is the first time that the Charlotte woman, who was recently released from an Atlanta hospital, has talked publicly about her experience. She and her husband, both missionaries, had been in Liberia for a year working in a clinic when she contracted the disease, September 3, 2014. (AP Photo/Bob Leverone)

"Our family is rejoicing over Kent's safe arrival, and we are confident that he is receiving the very best care," Amber Brantly said, adding that she was able to see her husband Sunday.

Brantly and Nancy Writebol served on the same mission team treating Ebola victims when they contracted the virus themselves. Brantly was serving as a physician in the hospital compound near Monrovia, Liberia, when he became infected. Writebol worked as a hygienist whose role included decontaminating those entering or leaving the Ebola treatment area at that hospital.

There is no cure for Ebola, which causes hemorrhagic fever that kills at least 60 percent of the people it infects in Africa. Ebola spreads through close contact with bodily fluids and blood, meaning it is not spread as easily as airborne influenza or the common cold. Africa's under-developed health care system and inadequate infection controls make it easier for the Ebola virus to spread and harder to treat.

Any modern hospital using standard infection-control measures should be able to handle it, and Emory's infectious disease unit is one of about four in the U.S. that is specially equipped to test and treat people exposed to the most dangerous viruses.

Patients are quarantined, sealed off from anyone who is not in protective gear. Lab tests are conducted inside the unit, ensuring that viruses don't leave the quarantined area. Family members can see and communicate with patients only through barriers.

Brantly arrived Saturday under stringent protocols, flying from West Africa to Dobbins Air Reserve base outside Atlanta in a small plane equipped to contain infectious diseases. A small police escort followed his ambulance to Emory, where he emerged dressed head to toe in white protective clothing and walked into the hospital on his own power.

A physician from Texas, Brantly is a Samaritan's Purse missionary. The Writebols are working through SIM USA. The two Christian organizations have partnered to provide health care in West Africa.

The Rev. John Munro, the Writebols' pastor at Calvary Church in Charlotte, North Carolina, described the couple as "quiet, unassuming people" who felt called by God" to go overseas 15 years ago.

Jeremy Writebol said his parents spent five years in Ecuador and nine years in Zambia before going to Liberia last August.

Munro added, "They take the Great Commission literally," a reference to the scriptural instruction from Jesus Christ to "make disciples of all nations."

Munro, whose church sponsors the Writebols' mission work, recalled speaking with the couple when the Ebola outbreak began. "We weren't telling them to come back; we were just willing to help them come back," he said. "They said, 'The work isn't finished, and it must continue.'"

The outbreak comes as nearly 50 African heads of state come to Washington, D.C., for the U.S.-Africa Leaders Summit — billed as a tool for African nations to integrate more into the world economy and community. With the outbreak, however, the presidents of Liberia and Sierra Leone have scrapped their plans to attend the three-day summit opening Monday.

Meanwhile, some airlines that serve West Africa have suspended flights, while international groups, including the Peace Corps, have evacuated some or all of their representatives in the region.

In the United States, public health officials continue to emphasize that treating Brantly and Writebol in the U.S. poses no risks to the public here.

"We know how to control it: hospital infection control and stopping it at the source in Africa," Dr. Tom Frieden, director of the U.S. Centers for Disease Control and Prevention, said, speaking Sunday on ABC's "This Week."

Frieden's agency is ramping up its effort to combat the outbreak. He promised "50 staff on the ground" in Liberia, Guinea and Sierra Leone "in the next 30 days."

### Isolation
Lagos, Nigeria
August 6, 2014
By The Associated Press

A Nigerian health official wearing a protective suit waits to screen passengers for the Ebola virus at the arrivals hall of Murtala Muhammed International Airport in Lagos, Nigeria. Six months into the biggest-ever Ebola outbreak, scientists say they've learned more about how the potentially lethal virus behaves and how future outbreaks might be stopped. The first cases of Ebola were reported in Guinea by the World Health Organization on March 23 before spreading to Sierra Leone, Liberia and elsewhere, August 4, 2014. (AP Photo/Sunday Alamba, File)

Nigerian authorities rushed to obtain isolation tents Wednesday, August 6, 2014 in anticipation of more Ebola infections as they disclosed five more cases of the virus and a death in Africa's most populous nation, where officials were racing to keep the gruesome disease confined to a small group of patients.

The five new Nigerian cases were all in Lagos, a megacity of 21 million people in a country already beset with poor health care infrastructure and widespread corruption, and all five were reported to have had direct contact with one infected man.

Meanwhile, the World Health Organization began a meeting to decide whether the crisis, the worst recorded outbreak of its kind, amounts to an international public health emergency. At least 932 deaths in four countries have been blamed on the illness, with 1,711 reported cases.

In recent years, the WHO has declared an emergency only twice, for swine flu in 2009 and polio in May. The declaration would probably come with recommendations on travel and trade restrictions and wider Ebola screening. It also would be an acknowledgment that the situation is critical and could worsen without a fast global response.

The group did not immediately confirm the new cases reported in Nigeria. And Nigerian authorities did not release any details on the latest infections, except to say they all had come into direct contact with the sick man who arrived by plane in Lagos late last month.

With the death toll mounting in the region, Liberia's president announced a state of emergency late Wednesday and said it may result in the suspension of some citizens' rights. She lamented that fear and panic had kept many family members from sending sick relatives to isolation centers.

"Ignorance and poverty, as well as entrenched religious and cultural practices, continue to exacerbate the spread of the disease," President Ellen Johnson Sirleaf said.

And in Sierra Leone, where enforcing quarantines of sick patients also has been met with resistance, some 750 soldiers deployed to the Ebola-ravaged east as part of "Operation Octopus."

Ebola, which causes some victims to bleed from the eyes, mouth and ears, can only be transmitted through direct contact with the bodily fluids of someone who is sick — blood, semen, saliva, urine, feces or sweat.

Millions in Lagos live in cramped conditions without access to flushable toilets. Signs posted across the city warn people not to urinate in public.

Kenneth Akihomi, a 47-year-old worker installing fiber-optic cable, said he was carefully washing his hands to avoid infection. But he said most people were relying on faith to stay healthy.

"They're not panicking. They are godly people," he said. "They believe they can pray, and maybe very soon there will be cure."

The revelation of more infections also came amid a public-sector doctors' strike in Nigeria that began in early July. So far, health workers monitoring the latest Ebola patients are still on the job.

Nigeria is the fourth West African country to be hit by the Ebola outbreak since it first emerged in March in the remote tropical forests of Guinea. The disease then spread to neighboring Sierra Leona and Liberia before reaching Nigeria, where it surfaced shortly before the government drew criticism for its response to the abduction of more than 200 schoolgirls by Islamic militants back in April. The girls are still missing.

Nigerian authorities said Tuesday, August 5, 2014 that doctors did not suspect Patrick Sawyer was suffering from Ebola when the 40-year-old Liberian-American arrived by plane late last month in Lagos, where the streets are a bewildering mix of wealth and abject poverty, awash in luxury SUVs and decrepit buses.

Sawyer, who worked for the Liberian government in Monrovia and had a wife and three young daughters in Minnesota, was on a business flight to Nigeria when he fell ill. Officials say a nurse who treated him has died and five others are sick with Ebola, including a doctor involved in his care.

West African countries pledged at a meeting in July to step up their surveillance at airports and borders following the start of the outbreak. But the early symptoms of Ebola — fever, muscle aches and vomiting — are similar to much more common tropical diseases such as malaria.

The specter of the virus spreading through Nigeria is particularly alarming, said Stephen Morse, an epidemiology professor at Columbia University's Mailman School of Public Health.

"It makes you nervous when so many people are potentially at risk," he said.

Authorities in Liberia said Sawyer's sister had recently died of Ebola, though Sawyer said he had not had close contact with her while she was ill.

In announcing Sawyer's death, Health Minister Onyebuchi Chukwu maintained late last month that Nigerian officials had been vigilant in isolating him.

"It was right there (at the airport) that the problem was noticed because we have maintained our surveillance," he told reporters. "And immediately, he went into the custody of the port health services of the federal ministry of health so there was no time for him to mingle in Lagos. He has not been in touch with any other person again since we took him from the airport."

Chukwu's comments were at odds with remarks made Tuesday by the Lagos state health commissioner, who said doctors did not suspect Ebola immediately and identified Sawyer as a possible case only after he had been hospitalized for about a day.

A Nigerian port health official uses a thermometer on a passenger at the arrivals hall of Murtala Muhammed International Airport in Lagos, Nigeria, August 6, 2014. (AP Photo/Sunday Alamba)

Sawyer, who had a fever and was vomiting on the plane, was coming from the infected country of Liberia but had a layover in Togo. As a result, officials may not have initially known his original point of departure, and it was unclear whether he was traveling on a Liberian or American passport.

Experts say people infected with Ebola can spread the disease only after they show symptoms. Since the incubation period can last up to three weeks, some of the Nigerians who treated Sawyer are only now showing signs of illness.

The national health minister on Wednesday said special tents would be used to establish isolation wards in all of Nigeria's states. Authorities were setting up an emergency center in Lagos to deal with Ebola and expected the facility to be "fully functional" by Thursday, he said.

Also Wednesday, the Spanish Defense Ministry said a medically equipped plane was ready to fly to Liberia to bring back a Spanish missionary priest who has Ebola. At the same time, Saudi officials reported a suspected Ebola death, underscoring the risk of the disease spreading by air travel even as many airlines curtail their flights to the most infected cities.

# 6

# Global Consequences

Protocol/FAQ
August 8, 2014
By Scott Mayerowitz
New York

Passenger Don Heim, right, of Alpharetta, Ga., is briefed by Transportation Security Administration trainer Byron Gibson before going through a new expedited security line at Hartsfield-Jackson International Airport in Atlanta. The news that a man flew from Liberia to the U.S. after exposure to Ebola, and wound up in a hospital isolation ward, has led to calls for tougher measures to protect Americans, such as a ban on flights from countries hit by the epidemic. Federal health officials and airlines have dismissed any risk to passengers who flew with the man last month and say they are protecting travelers by screening passengers and wiping down airplane cabins nightly, October 4, 2011. (AP Photo/David Goldman)

As the Ebola outbreak in West Africa worsens, airlines around the globe are closely monitoring the situation but have yet to make any drastic changes.

Below are some key questions about the disease, what airlines are doing and how safe it is to fly.

## Q: WHY ARE AIRLINES CONCERNED?

A: Airlines quickly take passengers from one part of the globe to another. With some germs, one sick passenger on a plane could theoretically infect hundreds of people who are connecting to flights to dozens of other countries. Health and airline officials note, however, that Ebola only spreads through direct contact. Outbreaks of diseases that can spread through the air, such as the flu and severe acute respiratory syndrome, or SARS, are more problematic for airlines.

## Q: SHOULD PEOPLE TRAVEL TO WEST AFRICA?

A: The Centers for Disease Control and Prevention issued a warning last week for Americans to avoid nonessential travel to West African nations with the outbreak.

## Q: IS EBOLA DEADLY?

A: Very much so. If contracted, there is no vaccine and no specific treatment. The World Health Organization on Friday said this is the largest and longest outbreak ever recorded of Ebola. About 1,700 people have been sickened in Guinea, Liberia, Sierra Leone and Nigeria; nearly 1,000 people have died.

## Q: HOW IS EBOLA TRANSMITTED?

A: The virus only spreads through direct contact with the blood or fluids of an infected person, according to the CDC. It can also be spread through objects, such as needles, that have been contaminated with infected fluids. No airborne transmission has been documented.

## Q: DO U.S. AIRLINES FLY TO WEST AFRICA?

A: Delta Air Lines flies to Dakar, Senegal; Accra, Ghana and Lagos, Nigeria. The airline also flies to Monrovia, Liberia, but for unrelated business reasons previously announced it will cancel that service at the end of September. Delta is letting passengers with flights to the region now until Aug. 15 push back travel until the end of the month. United Airlines also flies to Lagos, but has not issued any travel waiver. American Airlines does not fly to Africa.

## Q: WHAT ARE U.S. AIRLINES SAYING ABOUT IT?

A: There have been no flight cancelations. All three airlines said they are in regular communication with government agencies and health officials and will follow their recommendations.

## Q: WHAT ABOUT AIRLINES FROM OTHER COUN-TRIES?

A: European carriers such as Air France-KLM, British Airways and Lufthansa all fly to Western Africa from their hubs in Paris, Amsterdam, London and Frankfurt.

British Airways announced Tuesday that it is suspending flights to and from Liberia and Sierra Leone until Aug. 31 "due to the deteriorating public health situation in both countries."

Passengers with tickets can request a full refund or a flight at a later date. The only other airline, so far, to cancel any flights is the Middle East airline Emirates. It has suspended its service to Conakry, Guinea, until further notice. It is still flying to Dakar.

Lufthansa notes that "there is no risk of getting infected by the Ebola virus via air circulation during flight." Crews on Brussels Airlines flights have access to special thermoscans to check passengers' temperature, if they feel it's necessary.

Air France has put an Ebola plan into action that includes medical protection kits and disinfectant gel available to the crew. Passengers leaving Africa must fill out a questionnaire when entering the airport. They then have their temperature taken. They are only given a boarding pass if no symptoms are present.

## Q: ARE PASSENGERS LEAVING AFRICA BEING SCREENED?

A: Since the outbreak erupted, the CDC has sent about two dozen staffers in West Africa to help try to track cases, set up emergency response operations and provide other help to control the outbreak. Last week, CDC officials said the agency will send 50 more in the next month. CDC workers in Africa also are helping to screen passengers at airports, according to CDC director Dr. Tom Frieden.

## Q: ARE OTHER AIRPORTS SCREENING ARRIVING PASSENGERS?

A: Yes. Immigration and health officials at airports as far away as India, Australia, Russia, the Philippines, Myanmar, Macedonia and elsewhere are screening passengers for signs of sickness or elevated temperatures.

## Q: IS THE U.S. GOVERNMENT DOING ANYTHING EXTRA FOR ARRIVING PASSENGERS?

A: Border patrol agents at Washington's Dulles International Airport and New York's John F. Kennedy International Airport, in particular, are looking out for travelers who might have been exposed to the virus. They're watching for signs of fever, achiness, sore throat, stomach pain, rash or red eyes. The CDC also has staff at 20 U.S. airports and border crossings evaluating travelers with signs of dangerous infectious diseases and isolating them when necessary.

## Q: HAS THE AIRLINE INDUSTRY DEALT WITH ANY OUTBREAKS IN THE PAST?

A: In 2003, there was a global outbreak of severe acute respiratory syndrome, or SARS. The disease was first reported in Asia but quickly spread to more than two dozen countries in North America, South America and Europe. Unlike Ebola, SARS can spread when an infected person coughs or sneezes. During the 2003 outbreak, 8,098 people worldwide became sick with SARS; 774 of those died. Airports started screening incoming passengers for fever. The disease was devastating for airlines because fearful passengers stayed home.

Spain
Madrid
August 7, 2014
By The Associated Press

A Spanish missionary priest who tested positive for the Ebola virus was in stable condition at a Madrid hospital on Thursday, August 7, 2014 after being evacuated from Liberia, health officials said.

The priest, Miguel Pajares, 75, was helping to treat people infected with Ebola and was one of three who tested positive at the San Jose de Monrovia Hospital in Liberia earlier this week. He was flown to Spain on Thursday.

Juliana Bohi, an Equatorial Guinean nun with Spanish nationality who worked with him in Liberia, was also brought back but she is not infected.

Both worked for the San Juan de Dios hospital order, a Catholic humanitarian group that runs hospitals around the world.

An ambulance transporting Miguel Pajares, a Spanish priest who was infected with the Ebola virus while working in Liberia, leaves the Military Air Base of Torrejon de Ardoz, near Madrid, Spain, August 7, 2014. (AP Photo/Daniel Ochoa de Olza)

Both Pajares and Bohi were being kept in isolation at the Carlos III center in Madrid, which is run by La Paz hospital.

They arrived at a military air base near Madrid and were strapped to stretchers enclosed by transparent capsule-like tents that were pushed by personnel in protective white suits wearing masks. A convoy of ambulances took them to the hospital with a police escort.

Rafael Perez-Santamarina, director of Madrid's La Paz hospital, said that initial medical checks showed Pajares was in stable condition and Bohi was in good condition. He confirmed that neither was bleeding, which is a symptom of an advanced stage of the illness.

Bohi and two other missionaries working at the Liberian hospital tested negative. Officials said Bohi would be retested in Madrid and released if the result was once again negative.

Senior Madrid regional health official Antonio Alemany said Pajares didn't have a fever and the prognosis was good.

Ebola, which causes some victims to bleed from the eyes, mouth and ears, can only be transmitted through direct contact with the bodily fluids of someone who is sick — blood, semen, saliva, urine, feces or sweat.

The disease has no known cure. Alemany said Pajares was being kept hydrated but that if experimental treatment being tested in the United States on two Americans diagnosed with Ebola proved effective, Spain would seek to be able to use it.

It is the first time that someone infected with Ebola will be treated in Spain. A medically equipped Airbus 310 flew to Liberia on Wednesday to bring Pajares and Bohi to Spain.

Spain's Health Ministry said the case presented minimal risk to public health.

The other two aid workers who tested positive with Pajares were identified as Chantal Pascaline Mutwamene of Congo and Paciencia Melgar from Equatorial Guinea.

*Priest Miguel Pajares passed away on August 12, 2014*

## Economic Toll
Washington
August 9, 2014
By Paul Wiseman

Caterpillar has evacuated a handful of employees from Liberia. Canadian Overseas Petroleum Ltd. has suspended a drilling project. British Airways has canceled flights to the region. ExxonMobil and Chevron are waiting to see whether health officials can contain the danger.

The Ebola outbreak, which has claimed nearly 1,000 lives, is disrupting business and inflicting economic damage in the three African countries at the center of the crisis: Guinea, Sierra Leone and Liberia. So far, analysts say the crisis doesn't threaten the broader African or global economies.

"We must make sure it is controlled and contained as quickly as possible," said Olusegun Aganga, trade minister in Nigeria, which has confirmed nine cases of Ebola. "Once that is done, I don't think it will have a lasting impact on the economy."

The World Health Organization on Friday, August 8, 2014 declared the outbreak an international public health emergency. The WHO didn't recommend any travel or trade bans. But it cautioned anyone who had had close contact with Ebola patients to avoid international travel and urged exit screenings at international airports and border crossings.

The logo of Chevron is seen at a gas station downtown Los Angeles. As anxiety surrounding the Ebola crisis in Africa spread, economists say it's causing corporations to reassess their strategies and damaging the regional economy but so far causing no broader economic impact. Caterpillar and several mining companies have evacuated employees from Liberia. British Airlines has canceled flights to the region. Exxon and Chevron say they're waiting to see whether public health authorities can contain the Ebola outbreak in three West African countries, April 25, 2013. (AP Photo/Damian Dovarganes

"When you have a widespread outbreak of Ebola, you can end up with a panic," said John Campbell, senior fellow for Africa studies at the Council on Foreign Relations. "People won't go to work. Expatriates will leave. Economic activity will slow. Fields won't get planted."

The World Bank estimates that the outbreak will shrink economic growth in Guinea, where the crisis emerged in March, from 4.5 percent to 3.5 percent this year.

Ama Egyaba Baidu-Forson, an economist at IHS Global Insight who focuses on sub-Saharan Africa, is cutting her forecasts for growth this year in Liberia and Sierra Leone. She warned that prices would rise as food and other staples become scarce and that the region's already fragile governments would run up big budget deficits in fighting Ebola.

Baidu-Forson says the countries hit by Ebola ultimately could require financial help from the International Monetary Fund.

In the meantime, multinational companies that do business in the resource-rich region are scrambling to respond to the crisis. Among them:

— Heavy equipment manufacturer Caterpillar Inc., based in Peoria, Illinois, has "evacuated less than 10 people" from Liberia, company spokeswoman Barbara Cox said by email. In a statement, Caterpillar said: "The health and safety of our people is our top priority.... We will continue to monitor the situation closely."

— British Airways has announced that it's suspending flights to and from Liberia and Sierra Leone through Aug. 31 "due to the deteriorating public health situation in both countries."

— Tawana Resources, an Australian iron-ore company, said it had suspended "all non-essential field activities within Liberia" and sent all non-essential African workers, expatriates and contractors home.

— London-based mining company African Minerals has begun imposing health checks and travel restrictions on employees in the region.

— Canadian Overseas Petroleum, based in Calgary, has stopped drilling in Liberia. And some of its expatriate employees have left the country.

— ExxonMobil said in a statement that its offices remain open and that "we're taking precautions to ensure the health and safety of our employees." The company has offices in Liberia, Nigeria and several other African nations.

— Chevron, which has an office in the Liberian capital of Monrovia and is in the process of exploring for oil off Liberia's coast, said it's "closely monitoring the outbreak of Ebola virus in West Africa." But the company wouldn't say whether it was withdrawing any employees or taking any other steps as a result of the outbreak.

So far, the economic damage has not affected West Africa's biggest economy, Nigeria's, though the disease has already spread to that country.

"It's not stopped commerce; it's not stopped buying," said Danladi Verheijen, managing director of the investment firm Verod Capital. "The flights are still full going into Nigeria."

Timi Austen-Peters, chairman of the Nigerian engineering and manufacturing firm Dorman Long, met in Washington on Friday with investors who were interested in Africa. Ebola, he says, didn't come up in the discussion.

"We were having a good old-fashioned business meeting," he says. "They were not in any way spooked."

## Impossible Dilemma
Dakar, Senegal
August 13, 2014
By The Associated Press

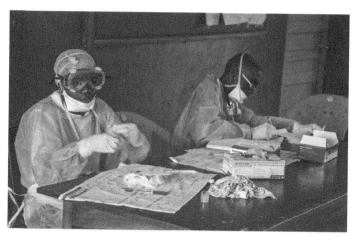

Health worker wearing protective clothing and equipment, out of fear for the deadly Ebola virus, sit at a desk at the Kenema Government Hospital situated in the Eastern Province in Kenema, 300 kilometers, (186 miles) from the capital city of Freetown, Sierra Leone. Over the decades, Ebola cases have been confirmed in 10 African countries, including Congo where the disease was first reported in 1976. But until this year, Ebola had never come to West Africa, August 9, 2014. (AP Photo/ Michael Duff)

Doctors treating a Sierra Leone physician with Ebola defended their decision not to give him an experimental drug, saying Wednesday, August 13, 2014 they feared it was too risky.

Calling it "an impossible dilemma," Doctors Without Borders explained in detail last month's decision in response to a New York Times story on the case. It would have been the first time the experimental drug was tried in humans.

The explanation came the same day that another top doctor from Sierra Leone died of the disease, further fueling a debate about how to apportion a limited supply of untested drugs and vaccines and whether they are even effective.

Ebola has killed more than 1,000 people and sickened nearly 2,000 in the current West African outbreak that has also hit Guinea, Liberia and Nigeria. Many of the dead are health workers, who are often working with inadequate supplies and protection.

At the time that the experimental treatment was being considered for Dr. Sheik Humarr Khan, his immune system was already starting to produce antibodies suggesting he might recover, Doctors Without Borders said in the statement. Khan was also due to be transferred to a European hospital that would be more capable of handling problems that might arise, it said.

The experimental drug, ZMapp, is designed to boost the immune system to help it fight the virus. Since Khan's body was already producing an immune response, the doctors may have feared that any boost would kick it into overdrive.

In the end, the treating physicians decided against using the drug. They never told Khan of its existence because they felt it would be unethical to tell him of a treatment they might not use. Shortly after their decision, however, Khan's condition worsened, the statement said, and the company providing the medical evacuation decided not to transfer him. He died a few days later, on July 29.

"Every day, doctors have to make choices, sometimes difficult, about treatment for their patients," said the Doctors Without Borders statement. "Trying an untested drug on patients is a very difficult decision, particularly in the light of the 'do no harm' principle."

ZMapp has since been given to two U.S. aid workers and a Spanish missionary priest. The Americans are improving, although it is unclear what role ZMapp has played in that, but the priest died Tuesday.

The last known doses of ZMapp arrived in Liberia on Wednesday, carried personally by Foreign Minister Augustine Ngafuan. The California-based company that makes the drug, Mapp Pharmaceuticals, has said that its supplies are now exhausted, and it will take months to produce even a modest amount.

The drug has never before been tested in humans, and it is not clear if it is effective or even harmful.

Dr. Moses Massaquoi, who helped the Liberian government acquire it, told reporters at the airport that there was enough to treat three people. Previously, the government had said it would only have enough to treat two sick doctors.

They would be the first Africans known to receive the treatment.

While many have called for more experimental drugs to be made available, noting that Ebola patients often have little to lose and so much to potentially gain, others have expressed caution.

"To use this drug without having any information on its human benefits or dangers runs the risk of mistakenly thinking it is either effective or not based upon anecdotal evidence, a difficulty that could prove disastrous for later in this outbreak or future ones," said Dr. Philip M. Rosoff, director of the Clinical Ethics Program at Duke University Hospital.

The maker of another experimental Ebola drug said Wednesday that it is not ready to make the treatment available. Canada's Tekmira Pharmaceuticals Corp. said it is continuing talks with governments and international agencies.

The Canadian government has promised to donate 800 to 1,000 doses of its untested Ebola vaccine to the World Health Organization.

Shelly Glover, the Canadian regional minister for Manitoba, where Canada's National Microbiology Laboratory is located, said Wednesday that the vaccines haven't left Canada yet. She said WHO is assembling a panel of experts to help decide who will get one.

Likely candidates are health care workers in Africa who are among the most vulnerable because of their close contact with Ebola patients.

Massaquoi, from Liberia, said negotiations for access to the vaccine are taking place now. Guinea is also considering asking for it.

Unlike ZMapp, which is being given to only a handful of people and is unlikely to yield significant information about the drug's effectiveness, the vaccine could be tested in a small, but more rigorous field trial.

"It gives us an opportunity to test the vaccine in an outbreak situation in populations that are at risk," said David Heymann, who professor at London School of Hygiene and Tropical Medicine.

Meanwhile, Nigeria confirmed that another person has died from Ebola, bringing the toll in that country to three. The man was under quarantine because he had contact with Patrick Sawyer, a Liberian-American who flew into Nigeria with the disease and died of it last month.

# 7

# The Long Road Ahead

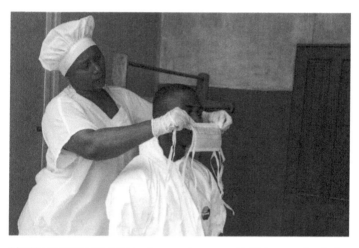

A healthcare worker, left, helps a colleague as she prepares his Ebola personal protective equipment before entering the Ebola isolation ward at Kenema Government Hospital, in Kenema, the Eastern Province around 300km, (186 miles), from the capital city of Freetown in Sierra Leone, August 12, 2014. (AP Photo/ Michael Duff)

### Death, Heat, Rumors
London
August 18, 2014
By The Associated Press

Doctors and nurses fighting Ebola in West Africa are working 14-hour days, seven days a week, wearing head-to-toe gear in the heat of muddy clinics. Agonizing death is the norm. The hellish conditions aren't the only problem: Health workers struggle to convince patients they're trying to help them, not hurt them.

Rumors are rife that Western aid workers are importing Ebola, stealing bodies or even deliberately infecting patients. Winning trust is made harder by a full suit of hood, goggles, mask and gown that hides their faces.

"You want to say so much ... because they're in so much pain," said nurse Monia Sayah, of Doctors Without Borders. "They suffer so much, but they can only see your eyes."

The outbreak has hit three of the world's poorest countries, where health systems there were already woefully understaffed and ill-equipped. In Liberia, there is only one doctor for every 100,000 people, while in Sierra Leone there are two, according to the World Health Organization; there were no statistics available for Guinea. The figure is 245 for the United States.

Emotional distress conspires with exhaustion and dehydration, but doctors say it's hard to stop working. "When the need is so great, you can't justify not being there for a day or going home earlier," said Dr. Robert Fowler, who recently worked in Guinea and Sierra Leone.

The critical care doctor at Sunnybrook Hospital in Toronto, Canada — now on sabbatical with the World Health Organization — said that the barrier of the protective suit is big but not insurmountable.

"There was a young girl, about 6, who came in late in the illness who was bleeding from her bowels, very dehydrated and delirious," he said. Ebola wiped out her immediate family — so she was all alone.

"She was very frightened and very reluctant to engage, and just wanted to push people away," he said. Fowler spent days trying to help her, bringing her things she wanted like Fanta soda. "She eventually developed this sense that this person in the suit who's a bit scary is trying to help me."

One day he brought the girl her favorite dish: cucumbers and lime. "She chowed down," he said — a sign that she was on the mend. Fowler said the girl was close to being discharged by the time he left Guinea.

The girl is the exception rather than the rule. Death is the fate of more than half of the West Africans infected in the Ebola outbreak.

"With the mortality rate being what it is," Fowler said, "you know every day there will be a couple of patients on your ward who didn't make it through the night."

Dr. Kent Brantly — an American who fell sick from Ebola last month treating patients — echoed Fowler in speaking of the moral weight of the struggle.

"I held the hands of countless individuals as this terrible disease took their lives away from them," Brantly said in a statement this month. "I witnessed the horror firsthand and I can still remember every face and name."

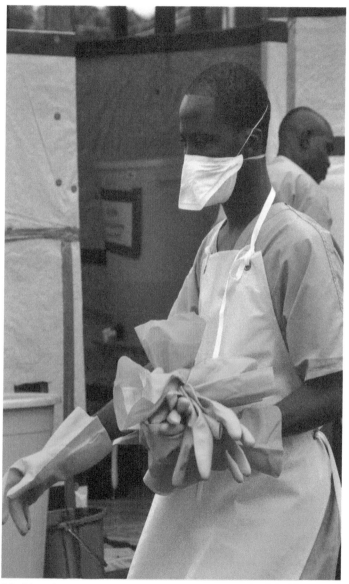

A health worker carries gloves at an Ebola treatment center in the city of Monrovia, Liberia. Liberia's armed forces were given orders to shoot people trying to illegally cross the border from neighboring Sierra Leone, which was closed to stem the spread of Ebola, local newspaper Daily Observer reported, August 18, 2014. (AP Photo/Abbas Dulleh)

Brantly is now being treated in an Atlanta hospital. His condition was improving.

Sayah, the nurse, said that heat makes it impossible to work continuously for more than an hour. It means tasks have to be completed with near-military precision. Her makeshift Ebola tent hospital in Gueckedou, southern Guinea, was converted from an earlier clinic set up by Doctors Without Borders to handle cholera epidemics.

"If you have to do patients' blood work and IVs, you focus only on this, and you know your other team members will get the patients food and drink," she said.

The tough odds don't make it easier to see a patient die.

"There was a very strong, resilient, gentleman, who always made an effort to sit up and open his eyes and tell us how grateful he was that we were here," said Sahah. She said the man appeared to be improving but suddenly deteriorated. She was forced to take a break after getting dehydrated. When he returned about 40 minutes later, he was dead.

"When a patient dies like that, it's very upsetting because we're their last hope."

Cokie van der Velde, a sanitation specialist for Doctors Without Borders in Guinea and Liberia, cleaned Ebola wards — washing floors, emptying buckets and collecting bodies.

One day, she came across a harrowing sight.

"I walked into a room with four bodies and they'd all died in the most grotesque positions, with a lot of blood and feces everywhere," she said. "During the night, one man had crawled to the door and the other people who died, they seemed to have fallen off their beds and were bent backwards."

Normally, the Briton spends her days in Yorkshire, England, tending to her garden and looking after her grandchildren. Van der Velde has worked on two previous Ebola outbreaks and says she does it because she believes in justice and equality.

She said the need for medical care is overwhelming in this outbreak because of the heavy toll Ebola has taken on health workers. Many of those sickened and killed have been doctors and nurses. That has sparked fear among local staffers and led to strikes and resignations.

"I can't blame them," van Der Velde said. "They're scared."

## Growing Unrest
Monrovia, Liberia
August 18, 2014
By Jonathan Paye-Layleh and Krista Larson

Liberian Police dressed in riot gear deploy at a MSF, 'Doctors Without Borders', Ebola treatment center as they provide security in the city of Monrovia, Liberia. Liberia's armed forces were given orders to shoot people trying to illegally cross the border from neighboring Sierra Leone, which was closed to stem the spread of Ebola, local newspaper Daily Observer reported, August 18, 2014. (AP Photo/Abbas Dulleh)

Authorities in Liberia urgently searched on Monday, August 18, 2014 for 17 people who fled an Ebola medical center over the weekend when it was attacked by looters who stole blood-stained sheets and mattresses and took them into an enormous slum.

Health officials were combing Monrovia's West Point area that is home to at least 50,000 people to try to stop the virus from spreading further in a country where more than 400 people already have died.

The World Health Organization on Monday urged Liberia and other Ebola-affected countries to screen all passengers leaving international airports, sea ports and major ground crossings.

Those with symptoms of the virus also were urged not to travel. Many airlines have halted services to the capitals of Liberia and neighboring Sierra Leone.

The weekend chaos in Monrovia highlights the growing unease and panic in Liberia amid the mounting Ebola death toll and illustrates the risks of further instability in this deeply impoverished country where mistrust of the government runs high. In addition, health workers are complaining about a lack of protective gear. Treatment centers are viewed by many as a place where people go just to die.

"They are not happy with the way Ebola is being managed and the response that the government is providing," said Koala Oumarou, country director for the aid group Plan Liberia, which is helping the health ministry to raise awareness. "It's where the frustration is coming from."

Liberia's president already has declared a state of emergency, dispatching armed soldiers to enforce quarantines of infected areas. But little was done Saturday to stoop looters from invading the Ebola quarantine center and taking items covered in bodily fluids that now could only further transmit the gruesome virus, witnesses said. Ebola is spread through direct contact with the blood, vomit, feces or sweat or sick people.

"This West Point situation really was our greatest setback since we started this fight, and we are working on making sure that we can correct that situation," Liberian Information Minister Lewis Brown told The Associated Press.

"We have learned a bit of bitter lesson here," he added.

Witnesses say an angry mob attacked the West Point facility, a "holding center" for people who had been exposed to Ebola and were being monitored during an incubation period for signs of the disease. The looters took medical equipment, and mattresses and sheets that had bloodstains, said a senior police official, who insisted on anonymity because he was not authorized to speak to journalists.

"All between the houses you could see people fleeing with items looted from the patients," the official said, adding that he now feared "the whole of West Point will be infected."

Witnesses said the weekend mob was angry about possible Ebola patients being brought into their area. None of those who fled had yet been confirmed to have Ebola, Assistant Health Minister Tolbert Nyenswah said.

The ransacking of the holding center is only the latest sign of anger among Liberians with the government's response to the crisis. Some health workers and burial teams also have faced aggression from communities who fear the corpses will sicken them. Others have held protests when bodies left on the streets have not been collected fast enough.

This year's outbreak marks the first time the gruesome disease has made its way to Liberia, presenting a herculean task for the aid workers trying to halt its spread through awareness campaigns. Despite the billboards and radio jingles, fear and denial have obstructed efforts to get the crisis under control, observers say.

Liberia is now the country with the highest number of Ebola deaths in the affected West African countries — 413 as of last week — and most believe even that figure is vastly under-estimated. Some of the hardest-hit areas of the country are under quarantine, and many victims are dying uncounted in their own homes, aid workers say.

On Monday, police in riot gear provided security at a new treatment center being operated by Doctors Without Borders, which is also known by its French acronym, MSF.

Lindis Hurum, MSF's project coordinator in Liberia, has described the conditions on the ground there as "catastrophic."

"I think it needs a massive intervention from the international community," she said Monday of the mounting crisis. "This is something that goes way beyond the Liberian government and local authorities, and beyond what MSF can do. The scale is so big now and I think it will get even worse than it is today."

### The Upper Hand
Monrovia, Liberia
August 27, 2014
By Jonathan Paye-Layleh

Ebola still has the "upper hand" in the outbreak that has killed more than 1,400 people in West Africa, but experts have the means to stop it, a top American health official said during a visit to the hardest-hit countries.

Dr. Tom Frieden, director of the U.S. Centers for Disease Control and Prevention, was in Liberia on Tuesday and later planned to stop in Sierra Leone and Guinea. Nigeria also has cases, but officials there have expressed optimism the virus can be controlled.

"Lots of hard work is happening. Lots of good things are happening," Frieden said at a meeting attended by Liberian President Ellen Johnson Sirleaf on Monday. "But the virus still has the upper hand."

A man, right, working for a humanitarian group, throws water in a small bag to West Point residents behind the fence of a holding area, as they wait for a second consignment of food from the Liberian Government to be handed out, at the West Point area, near the central city area of Monrovia, Liberia, August 22, 2014. (AP Photo/Abbas Dulleh)

Even as Liberia has resorted to stringent measures to try to halt Ebola's spread, frustration mounted over the slow collection of bodies from neighborhoods of Monrovia. A group of residents attached plastic ties to the wrists and ankles of one suspected Ebola victim and dragged his corpse to a busy street.

Authorities have decreed that all the dead must be collected by government health workers and cremated because contact with bodies can transmit the virus.

There is no proven treatment for Ebola, so health workers primarily focus on isolating the sick. But a small number of patients in this outbreak have received an experimental drug called ZMapp. The London hospital treating a British nurse infected in Sierra Leone, William Pooley, said he is now receiving the drug.

It was unclear where the doses for Pooley came from. The California-based maker of ZMapp has said its supplies are exhausted.

Two Americans, a Spaniard and three health workers in Liberia have received ZMapp. It is unclear if the drug is effective. The Americans have been released from the hospital, but the Spaniard died, as did a Liberian doctor.

In Nigeria, two more Ebola patients were declared to have recovered and were released from hospital, Health Minister Onyebuchi Chukwu said Tuesday. Five people have died of the disease in Nigeria, while a total of seven have recovered. One person remains in the hospital in an isolation ward, Chukwu said.

Meanwhile, the World Health Organization announced that it is pulling out its team from the eastern Sierra Leonean city of Kailahun, where an epidemiologist working with the organization was recently infected. Daniel Kertesz, the organization's representative in the country, said that the team was exhausted and that the added stress of a colleague getting sick could increase the risk of mistakes.

Also, Canadian health officials late Tuesday said in a statement that they would evacuate a three-member mobile laboratory team in Sierra Leone after people in their hotel were diagnosed with Ebola.

The outbreak is the largest on record. Doctors took a long time to identify it, it is happening in a region where people are highly mobile, it has spread to densely populated areas, and many people have resisted or hid from treatment. The disease has overwhelmed the already shaky health systems in some of the world's poorest countries.

"Ebola doesn't spread by mysterious means. We know how it spreads," Frieden said in remarks carried on Liberian TV. "So we have the means to stop it from spreading, but it requires tremendous attention to every detail."

Liberian officials have sealed off an entire slum neighborhood in the capital. Sirleaf also has declared a state of emergency and ordered all top government officials to remain in the country or return from any trips.

Late Monday, her office said in a statement that any officials who defied the order had been fired. The statement did not say how many or who had been dismissed.

According to WHO, the Ebola outbreak has killed over half of the more than 2,600 people sickened. The U.N. agency said an unprecedented 240 health care workers have been infected.

The agency attributed the high number of infections among health workers to a shortage of protective gear, improper use of such equipment, and a shortage of staff to treat the tremendous influx of patients.

A Liberian policeman warns residents of the West Point area to be calm, as they wait for a second consignment of food from the Liberian Government to be handed out, at the West Point area, near the central city area of Monrovia, Liberia, August 22, 2014. (AP Photo/Abbas Dulleh)

In the current outbreak, as many as 90,000 protective suits will be needed every month, according to Jorge Castilla, an epidemiologist with the European Union Commission's Department for Humanitarian Aid. He did not say how many suits were lacking.

The outbreak also desperately needs more workers to trace the people the sick have come into contact with and more centers where patients can be screened for the disease in a way that contains any Ebola infections, Castilla said.

An Ebola outbreak emerged over the weekend in Congo, though experts say it is not related to the West African epidemic. Doctors Without Borders, which is running many of the treatment centers in the West Africa outbreak, said it is sending experts and supplies to Congo but warned that the charity's resources are stretched thin.

# 8

# The Cure?

Dr. Tom Frieden, director of the U.S. Centers for Disease Control, holds a media briefing in Atlanta. The briefing included a public health assessment of the Ebola outbreak in West Africa, and an update on efforts to control the spread of the outbreak, September 2, 2014. (AP Photo/Alex Sanz)

## First Signs
Atlanta
August 29, 2014
By Marilynn Marchione

An experimental Ebola drug healed all 18 monkeys infected with the deadly virus in a study, boosting hopes that the treatment might help fight the outbreak raging through West Africa — once more of it can be made.

The monkeys were given the drug, ZMapp, three to five days after they were infected with the virus and when most were showing symptoms. That is several days later than any other experimental Ebola treatment tested so far.

The drug also completely protected six other monkeys given a slightly different version of it three days after infection in a pilot test. These two studies are the first monkey tests ever done on ZMapp.

"The level of improvement was utterly beyond my honest expectation," said one study leader, Gary Kobinger of the Public Health Agency of Canada in Winnipeg.

"For animal data, it's extremely impressive," said Dr. Anthony Fauci, director of the National Institute of Allergy and Infectious Diseases, which had a role in the work.

It's not known how well the drug would work in people, who can take up to 21 days to show symptoms and are not infected the way these monkeys were in a lab.

Several experts said it's not possible to estimate a window of opportunity for treating people, but that it was encouraging that the animals recovered when treated even after advanced disease developed.

The study was published online Friday by the journal Nature.

ZMapp had never been tested in humans before two Americans aid workers who got Ebola while working in Africa were allowed to try it. The rest of the limited supply was given to five others.

There is no more ZMapp now, and once a new batch is ready, it still needs some basic tests before it can be tried again during the African outbreak, Fauci said. "We do need to know what the proper dose is" in people and that it's safe, he said.

Ebola has killed more than 1,500 people this year and the World Health Organization says there could be as many as 20,000 cases before the outbreak is brought under control. On Friday, it spread to a fifth African country — Senegal, where a university student who traveled there from Guinea was being treated.

There is no approved vaccine or specific treatment, just supportive care to keep them hydrated and nourished. Efforts have focused on finding cases and tracking their contacts to limit the disease, which spreads through contact with blood and other fluids.

ZMapp is three antibodies that attach to cells infected with Ebola, helping the immune system kill them.

Of the seven people known to have been treated with ZMapp, two have died — a Liberian doctor and a Spanish priest. The priest received only one of three planned doses. The two Americans recovered, as have two Africans who received ZMapp in Liberia — a Congolese doctor and a Liberian physician's assistant who were expected to be released from a treatment center on Saturday. A British nurse also got the drug, reportedly the two unused doses left over from treating the Spanish priest.

Doctors have said there is no way to know whether ZMapp made a difference or the survivors recovered on their own, as about 45 percent of people infected in this outbreak have.

ZMapp's maker, Mapp Biopharmaceutical Inc., of San Diego, has said the small supply of the drug is now exhausted and that it will take several months to make more. The drug is grown in tobacco plants and was developed with U.S. government support.

Kobinger said it takes about a month to make 20 to 40 doses at a Kentucky plant where the drug is being produced. Officials have said they are looking at other facilities and other ways to ramp up production, and Kobinger said there were plans for a clinical trial to test ZMapp in people early next year.

The monkey study involved scientists from the Canada health agency, Mapp Biopharmaceutical, the U.S. National Institutes of Health and the United States Army Medical Research Institute of Infectious Disease.

Eighteen monkeys were given lethal amounts of Ebola in a shot, then received three intravenous doses of ZMapp, given three days apart starting three to five days after they were infected. Some were showing severe symptoms such as excessive bleeding, rashes and effects on their liver.

All treated with ZMapp survived; three other infected monkeys who did not get the drug died within eight days.

Primates have been good stand-ins for people for many viral diseases, but how well they predict human responses to Ebola, "we just don't know," said Dr. Cameron Wolfe, a Duke University infectious disease specialist. The study also "tells us nothing about side effects" people might have, he added.

Still, it was encouraging that even monkeys with severe symptoms got better, said Wolfe and Erica Ollmann Saphire, a Scripps Research Institute professor who has worked with some of the study leaders on antibodies to Ebola.

"The treatment window in humans needs to be established in a well-controlled trial" that also would explore the correct dose of ZMapp in people, Saphire wrote in an email. "Given its tremendous efficacy in the nonhuman primates, I don't see how it couldn't be helpful in people."

Praise
Monrovia, Liberia
August 30, 2014
By Jonathan Paye-Layleh

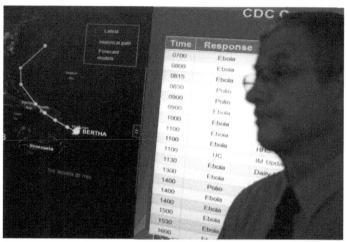

Steve Monroe, deputy director of the National Center for Emerging and Zoonotic
Infectious Diseases at the U.S. Centers for Disease Control and Prevention, stands next
to a response activity board during an interview at the agency's Emergency Operations
Center, in Atlanta. An American aid worker infected with Ebola arrived Tuesday from
Liberia to Emory University Hospital, just downhill from the CDC, joining a second patient
being given an experimental treatment that has never before been tested on humans,
August 5, 2014. (AP Photo/David Goldman)

A Liberian health worker who recovered from Ebola after receiving an experimental drug urged the manufacturer to speed up its production and send it to Africa, while crowds celebrated in the streets Saturday after authorities reopened a slum that had been barricaded for more than a week to try to contain the disease.

Physician's assistant Kyndy Kobbah was expected to be released from hospital Saturday after she survived Ebola, which has been fatal in more than half the cases sweeping West Africa. Kobbah contracted the disease while working at a government-run hospital north of the capital.

In an interview with The Associated Press before her release, she said when she informed her family that she had been cured, the home exploded with joy "and the house is on fire right now" with celebration.

"I am very fine and all right, glory be to God," she said. "I trusted God that I was going to be healed."

Kobbah urged the manufacturer of the experimental drug known as ZMapp to step up production. The company has said that all its supplies are exhausted and it will take months to make more.

"They need to make more Zmapp and send to us," she said.

Doctors have said there is no way to know whether ZMapp made a difference or if survivors like Kobbah recovered on their own, as about 45 percent of people infected in this outbreak have. The drug had never been tested in humans before it was given to two Americans who were infected with Ebola in Liberia. They survived Ebola and were released from an Atlanta hospital.

However, a study released online Friday by the journal Nature found that ZMapp healed all 18 monkeys infected with the deadly virus.

Meanwhile, tensions diminished Saturday in the West Point neighborhood of Liberia's capital after authorities lifted a blockade that had sparked unrest. Residents living in the area had feared running out of food and safe water on the peninsula.

Liberia's president had ordered the barricade on Aug. 19 after West Point residents stormed an Ebola health center several days earlier. Residents said they did not want sick people being brought into the community, although those staying at the center were only under observation during a 21-day incubation period.

Amid the melee, some protesters made off with blood-stained mattresses and other materials that could potentially spread the Ebola virus.

Lifting the quarantine Saturday morning doesn't mean there is no Ebola in the West Point slum, said Information Minister Lewis Brown. Authorities, though, are more confident now that they can work with residents to screen for the sick, he said.

"They're comfortable with the way the leadership and the community is working with the health team to make sure that the community remains safe," he said.

Liberia has been the hardest hit of the five countries with Ebola cases in West Africa, reporting at least 694 deaths among 1,378 cases. More than 3,000 cases have been reported across Liberia, Guinea, Sierra Leone and Nigeria, and on Friday Senegal announced its first case.

A student from Guinea who had been missing for several weeks showed up at a hospital in Dakar on Tuesday, seeking treatment but concealing that he had been in contact with other Ebola victims, Health Minister Awa Marie Coll Seck confirmed.

The next day, an epidemiological surveillance team in neighboring Guinea alerted Senegalese authorities that they had lost track of a person they were monitoring three weeks earlier, and that the person may have crossed into Senegal.

The student was tracked down in the Dakar hospital where he was confirmed with Ebola and immediately put into isolation where he is reported to be in satisfactory condition, Seck said. Authorities also sent out a team to disinfect the home where he was staying in Senegal.

## We Need Boosters
Washington
September 7, 2014
By Lauren Neegaard

New monkey studies show that one shot of an experimental Ebola vaccine can trigger fast protection, but the effect waned unless the animals got a booster shot made a different way. Some healthy people are rolling up their sleeves at the National Institutes of Health for the first human safety study of this vaccine in hopes it eventually might be used in the current Ebola outbreak in West Africa.

The NIH on Sunday published some of the key animal research behind those injections. One reason the vaccine was deemed promising was that a single dose protected all four vaccinated monkeys when they were exposed to high levels of Ebola virus just five weeks later, researchers reported in the journal Nature Medicine.

Is five weeks fast enough?

That's in line with other vaccines routinely used today, and fortunately it didn't take multiple doses to trigger that much protection, said Dr. Anthony Fauci, director of NIH's National Institute of Allergy and Infectious Diseases, whose employees led the work. The bigger challenge is that the protection wanes over time.

Researchers exposed monkeys to Ebola 10 months after vaccination, and this time only half were protected.

Partial protection is better than none, Fauci said. But the goal is long-lasting protection, so it was time to try booster shots. The vaccine is made with a chimpanzee cold virus, used as a delivery system for pieces of an Ebola gene.

The researchers tried simply giving another dose as a booster two months later. That didn't work well enough.

Seen through a window, U.S. Centers for Disease Control and Prevention officials sit in on a conference call about Ebola with CDC team members deployed in West Africa from the agency's Emergency Operations Center, August 5, 2014. (AP Photo/David Goldman)

So they tried a different approach called "prime-boost." The first dose, to prime the immune system, was that original chimp virus-based Ebola vaccine. But for the booster two months later, they made vaccine a different way. They encased the same Ebola gene pieces inside a poxvirus that's used to make a vaccine against smallpox. (Neither vaccine type can cause Ebola.)

This time, all four monkeys still were protected 10 months after the initial shot.

With the Ebola crisis rapidly worsening, the World Health Organization said Friday that it would try to speed the use of certain experimental products, including two vaccine candidates. The WHO said that in November, it expects early results from first-stage studies to see if the vaccine appears safe and triggers an immune reaction in people. That would help determine whether to test the shots' effectiveness in health care workers in West Africa.

Small animal and human safety studies cannot guarantee that experimental vaccines really work in an outbreak, Fauci said. That's why he emphasizes public health measures such as isolating the sick, quarantine and, especially for health workers, using personal protection equipment. "Make sure people do what works," he said.

The booster-shot findings illustrate an added complexity to speeding an experimental vaccine into the field. The initial first phase study results would shed light only on that "priming" vaccine made from the chimp cold virus, Fauci said. The poxvirus booster step would be tested later only if scientists decided the initial vaccine was promising enough.

Still, manufacturer GlaxoSmithKline has said it plans to begin manufacturing up to 10,000 doses of the initial NIH-developed vaccine. Canadian researchers created a similar Ebola vaccine that works in monkeys. Manufacturer NewLink Genetics of Ames, Iowa, said first-stage safety testing in healthy volunteers is set to begin in a few weeks.

## American Gets Blood from Fellow Ebola Survivor
Omaha, Nebraska
September 12, 2014
By Josh Funk, Jeff Martin & Mike Stobbe

An American aid worker infected with Ebola has been given blood from a fellow doctor who battled the disease, and Nebraska doctors say the man has responded well to aggressive treatment in the past week. Dr. Rick Sacra received two blood transfusions from Dr. Kent Brantly last weekend after arriving at the Nebraska Medical Center, Dr. Phil Smith said Thursday. Sacra also has been given an experimental drug that doctors refuse to identify, and he has received supportive care including IV fluids. Sacra is close friends with Brantly, one of the first two Americans treated for Ebola in Atlanta last month, from their missionary work.

"It really meant a lot to us that he was willing to give that donation so quickly after his own recovery," Sacra's wife, Debbie, said. Sacra, 51, and Brantly, 33, both arrived at the hospital in Omaha last Friday. Brantly tried to visit with Sacra over a video conference after he donated his blood to the hospital's blood bank for testing, but Debbie Sacra said Thursday her husband doesn't remember that encounter. The blood was reduced to plasma before the first transfusion.

These blood transfusions are believed to help a patient fight off the Ebola virus because the survivor's blood carries antibodies for the disease. More than 2,200 people have died in West Africa during the current Ebola outbreak, although Ebola hasn't been confirmed as the cause of all those deaths. Debbie Sacra said she hopes her husband's illness and the experience of other aid workers can lead to new treatments for Ebola before the outbreak spreads beyond West Africa. Rick Sacra, who had been working at a hospital in Liberia with the North Carolina-based charity SIM, was the third American aid worker with the Ebola virus to be flown to the U.S. for treatment.

Smith said doctors wanted to treat Sacra aggressively to give him the best chance of recovering. But he said that makes it hard to determine what is helping him improve. "We administered everything we had access to," Smith said. The doctors treating Sacra are talking with doctors at Emory University

Hospital who have treated two previous Ebola patients and are currently treating another Ebola patient. They hope to develop new treatments based on their experiences. Officials announced Thursday that Microsoft Corp. co-founder Paul Allen's foundation is donating $9 million to help the U.S. government fight the disease in West Africa. The grant to the CDC Foundation will help establish emergency operations centers to better track and respond to Ebola. A fourth American with Ebola arrived Tuesday at Emory in Atlanta. Few details have been released about that patient.

But the World Health Organization said a doctor who had been working in an Ebola treatment center in Sierra Leone tested positive for the disease and was to be evacuated Monday in stable condition. Debbie Sacra said her husband seemed about 80 percent normal mentally when she talked to him Thursday. She said that was a big improvement compared to last weekend. She said she knows her husband will be eager to return to West Africa "when he gets his strength back."

Debbie Sacra, wife of ebola patient Dr. Richard Sacra, laughs as she answers a question at a news conference held at the Nebraska Medical Center in Omaha, Neb. Dr. Phil Smith said Thursday that Sacra was responding well to aggressive treatment he received in the past week, including blood transfusions from a fellow doctor who also had Ebola, September 11, 2014. (AP Photo/Nati Harnik)

# 9

# The World Reacts

Bolivia's President Evo Morales, left, and Venezuela's President Nicolas Maduro, meet with reporters after the inauguration of the ALBA summit about Ebola in Havana, Cuba, October 20, 2014. (AP Photo/Ismael Francisco/ Cubadebate)

### Maduro and the Conspiracy Theory
Caracas, Venezuela
September 18, 2014
By Jorge Rueda,

President Nicolas Maduro accused CNN and other international media on Thursday, September 18, 2014, of conspiring against his government by publishing what he called false reports of a mysterious illness.

The head of the college of physicians in the city of Maracay sounded an alarm last week after reporting that eight people had died of unknown causes hours after checking into a hospital with common symptoms including high fevers and blotches on their skin.

Authorities immediately accused the doctor of lying and said all causes of deaths had been determined. But that didn't stop some Venezuelans, especially government opponents, from taking to social media to denounce the outbreak as an unknown epidemic and even speculating that the Ebola virus that has killed hundreds in West Africa had arrived on South America's shores.

The health scare has since cooled, but Maduro said he won't tolerate any "psychological terror" from foreign media that he accuses of misreporting the deaths.

While he named a number of media outlets for sowing panic, including the Miami Herald and the BBC's Spanish-language service, the president said he was considering pursuing legal action against CNN en Espanol, which devoted an entire program to the deaths. The network has yet to comment.

"These acts must be severely punished," Maduro said in an address broadcast on national TV and radio. "Venezuela in the past few hours, the past few days, has received attacks like we haven't seen in 15 years of revolution."

Partly fueling Venezuelans concerns is a dramatic increase in mosquito-borne illnesses around the Caribbean. The Health Ministry reported Wednesday that so far this year it has detected 398 cases of chikungunya virus and more than 45,745 people infected with dengue.

Both diseases rarely prove fatal when detected early. But Venezuela's economic problems have led to widespread shortages of medical supplies and medicines, making it harder for physicians to treat patients.

## Prayer and Evacuation Drill
Vatican City
September 24, 2014
By The Associated Press,

Pope Francis is urging international assistance to fight the Ebola virus in Africa.

Francis also urged the 30,000 people who attended his weekly general audience to pray for the victims.

It was the second time in as many days that Francis has raised the alarm about Ebola and called for international assistance to care for those affected.

He issued a similar appeal Tuesday, September 23, 2014 during a meeting with bishops visiting from Ghana.

At the Pratica Di Mare Air Base in Italy, The patient, a slight woman in her 30s, lay motionless on the stretcher as a half-dozen men in biohazard suits transferred her from a C-27J cargo plane into an ambulance and then into a mobile hospital isolation ward, never once breaking the plastic seal encasing her.

Pope Francis arrives for his weekly general audience in St. Peter's Square at the Vatican, September 24, 2014. (AP Photo/Alessandra Tarantino)

The exercise put on Wednesday was just a simulation of the procedures that would be used to evacuate an Ebola patient to Italy. But for Italian military, Red Cross and health care workers, it offered essential experience, especially for those on the front lines of the country's sea-rescue operation involving thousands of African migrants who arrive here every day in smugglers' boats.

Italian authorities and medical experts insist that the risk of Ebola spreading from Africa to Europe is small, given that the virus only spreads by direct contact with infected blood or other bodily fluids. They say Italy's first case of Ebola will probably be an Italian doctor or missionary who contracts the disease while caring for patients in Liberia, Sierra Leone or Guinea — the three hardest-hit countries — and is airlifted home for treatment.

Yet concern runs high: EU health ministers who met this week in Milan spent an entire session discussing Ebola and the EU. They concluded that, while the risk of the disease coming to Europe is low, the EU must improve coordination and prevention measures to better diagnose, transport and treat suspected cases.

"There is an emergency," said Dr. Natale Ceccarelli, who heads the infirmary at the Pratica di Mare air force base south of Rome, where the training course was staged. "If one person is infected, he infects everyone."

Ceccarelli has already flown once to an Italian navy transport ship taking part in the Mare Nostrum rescue operation after a would-be refugee who was picked up at sea was flagged during a routine health screening.

The patient was airlifted in one of the same self-contained mobile isolation units used for the defense ministry's simulation drill. He went first to Sicily and then to Rome aboard a C-130 transport plane and was taken immediately to the capital's Spallanzani hospital, which specializes in infectious diseases.

It turned out he had monkeypox, a virus similar to smallpox, not Ebola.

Ebola is believed to have infected more than 5,800 people in Liberia, Sierra Leone, Guinea, Nigeria and Senegal. Compared with swine flu, the number of infections is relatively small. But the World Health Organization has declared the outbreak an international public health emergency, and U.S. President Barack Obama has ordered up to 3,000 troops to be deployed to West Africa to build field hospitals and train medical staff.

Britain and France — which both have colonial ties to the region — have pledged to build treatment centers in Sierra Leone and Guinea. Italy has pledged to build a 90-bed treatment center in Sierra Leone, send experts from Spallanzani and give 1.5 million euros for the WHO to buy equipment and medicine.

Italy also has isolation units developed by a British engineer that are big enough for doctors to stabilize a patient on long-haul flights. Physicians can attach intravenous drips through the plastic sheeting without breaking the protective seal or even intubate a patient. Other European countries use smaller, simpler units that are suitable only for short flights, Ceccarelli said.

"It's very nice to have that option," said Dr. Benjamin Neuman, a virologist at the University of Reading in Britain. "Right now, there's a limited range" for transport, preventing patients with late-stage Ebola from being evacuated if the distances are too long or if they are already vomiting blood or suffering from diarrhea.

Italy has had the units on hand since 2005 and has used them 11 times to extract Italians suffering from dengue in Congo and hemorrhagic fever in Nepal, said Lt. Col. Marco Lastillo, an air force medic. The defense ministry stages the training courses twice a year, but added this extra session at the request of the health ministry because of the Ebola threat.

"This capacity that we have created for ourselves should be put to everyone's disposition," Defense Minister Roberta Pinotti told reporters at the base after watching the students perform the biohazard evacuation drill. She insisted that Italy's migrant crisis posed no particular Ebola threat, saying the medical screenings done in the Mare Nostrum operation would prevent any infected people from reaching the general population.

One of the students taking the course was Massimo Mazzieri, a volunteer with the Knights of Malta, the Catholic association that has a medical-relief corps working in war zones and natural disasters around the world, and with African migrants arriving in Italy. He and his classmates staged the drill, meticulously making sure the patient was passed from mobile isolation unit to mobile isolation unit without breaking the seal holding her germs inside.

"In this particular moment, Ebola is really on our minds, maybe a bit excessively," he said. "But we are ready."

## Urging the World
Washington
September 25, 2014
By Julie Pace

President Barack Obama, in a sober assessment of international efforts to stem a deadly Ebola outbreak, warned a high-level United Nations gathering Thursday that there is a "significant gap" between what's been offered so far and what is actually needed to stem the health crises in West Africa.

The leaders of the hardest-hit nations also appealed for more help, with the president of Sierra Leone calling the Ebola virus "worse than terrorism."

The emergency U.N. session on Ebola reflected the deep concern about an outbreak that has so far killed nearly 3,000 people. U.S. health officials have warned that the number of infected people could explode to at least 1.4 million by mid-January, though they have also cautioned that the totals could peak well below that if efforts to control the outbreak are ramped up.

Despite the grim warnings, Obama said international aid simply is not flowing into West Africa fast enough.

President Barack Obama speaks at the Centers for Disease Control and Prevention (CDC) in Atlanta. Obama traveled to the CDC, to address the Ebola crisis and announced that he is sending 3,000 American troops to West Africa nations fight the spread of the Ebola epidemic, September 16, 2014. (AP Photo/Pablo Martinez Monsivais)

"The outbreak is such where at this point, more people will die," Obama said as he closed out three days of diplomacy at the annual gathering of the U.N. General Assembly. "So this is not one where there should be a lot of wrangling and people waiting to see who else is doing what. Everybody has got to move fast in order for us to make a difference."

On Thursday, September 25, 2014, top lawmakers in Congress also approved the use of leftover Afghanistan war money to begin funding Obama's $1 billion request to help fight the outbreak.

Obama has come under criticism from some in West Africa for a slow response to the outbreak. He outlined a more robust plan last week, announcing that the U.S. would dispatch 3,000 U.S. troops to Liberia to set up facilities and form training teams to help with the response. The Pentagon mission will involve airlifting personnel, medical supplies and equipment, such as tents to house Ebola victims and isolate people exposed to the virus.

European Commission chief Jose Manuel Barroso announced Thursday that the European Union was increasing aid to tackle the outbreak by nearly $40 million.

The Ebola outbreak has hit Sierra Leone, Liberia and Guinea the hardest, leaving aid groups in the region have scrambled desperately for resources.

"Our 150-bed facility in Monrovia opens for just 30 minutes each morning. Only a few people are admitted, to fill beds made empty by those who died overnight," the president of Doctors Without Borders, Joanne Liu, told the U.N. meeting.

As leaders from West Africa appealed for more help from the international community, they also cast the outbreak as far more than a health crisis.

Liberian President Ellen Johnson Sirleaf, addressing the conference via video, cited a "precipitous decline in economic activity" as well as the "loss of income and jobs" for people in her country.

President Ernest Bai Koroma of Sierra Leone, who also spoke on a video feed, said his country was facing "life and death challenges" that were worse than the threat of terrorism. His comments appeared to be a veiled reference to the degree to which the threat from Middle East extremists — most notably the Islamic State group in Iraq and Syria — has dominated the discussions at the U.N. this week.

Koroma took the dramatic step Thursday of sealing off districts where more than 1 million live in order to try to contain the outbreak.

The fears around the outbreak have spread far beyond West Africa, and one African leader made a plaintive appeal Thursday during his address at the U.N. for the world not to stigmatize the entire continent.

"Not all countries in Africa have disease," Tanzanian President Jakaya Kikwete said, to rare applause from the chamber. "In fact, the affected countries are closer to Europe than they are to Kenya, Tanzania or South Africa in eastern and southern Africa. ... To cancel visits to these parts of Africa is incomprehensible."

While Obama touted the assistance the U.S. is providing, he said America alone cannot solve the problem and urged other nations to take similar action. "We don't have the capacity to do all of this by ourselves," he said. "We don't have enough health workers by ourselves. We can build the infrastructure and the architecture to get help in, but we're going to need others to contribute."

# 10

# At Risk

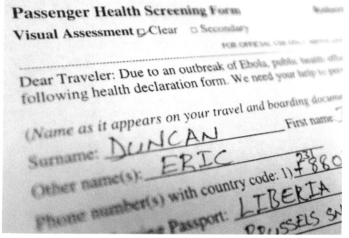

This photo shows a copy of a passenger health screening form filled out by Ebola patient Thomas Eric Duncan, which was obtained by the Associated Press from the Liberia Airport Authority. Liberia plans to prosecute Duncan, who brought Ebola into the U.S., alleging that he lied on a health questionnaire about not having any contact with an infected person, authorities said, October 2, 2014. (AP Photo/Kiichiro Sato)

Eric Duncan
Dallas, TX
October 8, 2014
By The Associated Press,

The death of the first Ebola patient diagnosed in the United States renewed questions about his medical care and whether Thomas Eric Duncan's life could have been extended or saved if the Texas hospital where he first sought help had taken him in sooner.

Duncan died in Dallas on Wednesday, October 8, 2014, a little more than a week after his illness exposed gaps in the nation's defenses against the disease and set off a scramble to track down anyone exposed to him.

The 42-year-old Liberian man had been kept in isolation since Sept. 28 at Texas Health Presbyterian Hospital, where a fevered Duncan first showed up days earlier and told the staff he had been in West Africa.

Doctors initially sent him home. He returned after his condition worsened.

Dr. Phil Smith is the director of the biocontainment center at the Nebraska Medical Center, where an NBC News freelance cameraman is being treated for Ebola. He said getting early treatment is key to survival.

When a patient reaches the point of needing dialysis and respiratory help, as Duncan did this week, there may be little doctors can do.

"At that point, any kind of intervention, whether it is an antiviral drug or convalescent plasma, is less likely to work," said Smith, an infectious disease specialist.

Duncan carried the deadly virus with him from his home in Liberia, though he showed no symptoms when he left for the United States. He arrived in Dallas on Sept. 20 and fell ill several days later.

Of the six Ebola patients treated so far in the U.S., Duncan was the only one not cared for in one of the special hospital units set up to deal with highly dangerous germs. That's because health officials knew the others had Ebola at the time they decided where the patients should go, whereas Duncan sought care at Texas Health Presbyterian hospital on his own.

Health officials also have said that any hospital with isolation capabilities can treat Ebola patients, but Duncan's death is sure to renew attention on the hospital's response.

There is no way to know whether any specific treatment or step might have saved Duncan's life. At the time of his death, he was taking an experimental antiviral drug.

He died "despite maximal interventions," said Dr. Tom Frieden, director of the Centers for Disease Control and Prevention. "The earlier someone is diagnosed, the more likely they will be to survive."

Pastor George Mason of Wilshire Baptist Church in Dallas was present when county officials told Louise Troh, the woman Duncan had been staying with, of his death.

"She expressed all the what-ifs," including whether the initial delay in admitting Duncan made a difference, Mason said.

Others in Dallas are still being monitored as health officials try to contain the virus that has ravaged West Africa, with about 3,800 people reported dead. The disease can be spread only through direct contact with the bodily fluids of an already sick person.

A hazardous material cleaner removes a wrapped item from the Dallas apartment where Thomas Eric Duncan, the Ebola patient who traveled from Liberia to Dallas, stayed. Workers packed the apartment into140 55-gallon drums. The contents were burned but the ashes remain in limbo. Louisiana officials have asked a judge to block Duncan's waste from entering the state. A hearing is scheduled, November 5, 2014. (AP Photo/LM Otero, File)

Health officials have identified 10 people, including seven health workers, who had direct contact with Duncan while he was contagious. Another 38 people also may have come into contact with him. The four people living in the Dallas apartment where Duncan stayed were moved to another home and are in isolation.

Officials have said everyone who had potential contact with Duncan is being monitored for 21 days, the maximum incubation period for the disease, which can cause vomiting, diarrhea, bleeding and in later stages, damage to vital organs.

Also Wednesday, a sheriff's deputy who went into the apartment where Duncan had stayed was hospitalized "out of an abundance of caution" after falling ill, authorities said.

Federal and state health officials say there's no indication the deputy had any direct contact with Thomas Eric Duncan.

Duncan's illness has stoked anxiety in some parts of Dallas. Several residents of the neighborhood where Duncan got sick told city officials they had been sent home from work. Some community volunteers shunned a nearby after-school program. And the hospital acknowledged that some patients were staying away out of fear of Ebola.

Duncan went to the emergency room of Texas Health Presbyterian in Dallas on Sept. 25, but was sent home. By Sept. 28, his condition had worsened and an ambulance took him back to the hospital.

Duncan's family visited the hospital earlier this week and got a glimpse of Duncan using a camera system. But relatives said Tuesday that they declined to view him again because the first time had been too upsetting.

"What we saw was very painful. It didn't look good," Duncan's nephew, Josephus Weeks, said Tuesday.

The hospital has changed its explanation several times about when Duncan arrived and what he said about his travel history. The hospital has said the staff did not initially suspect Ebola, even though Duncan told them on his first visit that that he came from West Africa.

His body was to be cremated and his remains returned to the family. The Centers for Disease Control recommends that bodies of Ebola victims not be embalmed and instead suggests they be cremated or promptly buried in a hermetically sealed casket.

Princess Duo, left, and Mamie Mangoe, right, both natively of Liberia who now live in Dallas, stand holding lit candles as they pray during a service at Wilshire Baptist Church that was dedicated to Thomas Eric Duncan, in Dallas. Nearly 150 persons attended the service for Duncan who died Wednesday of complication from Ebola, October 8, 2014. (AP Photo/Tony Gutierrez)

## The Risk of Hospital Staffs
### Dallas, TX
### October 14, 2014
### By Martha Mendoza

A sign points to the emergency room entrance at Texas Health Presbyterian Hospital in Dallas. The hospital has apologized for initially sending home a sick Thomas Eric Duncan, who told an emergency room nurse he'd recently arrived from West Africa, and temporarily spiked a 103-degree fever shortly before discharge. Two days later when he returned, sicker, Duncan tested positive for Ebola. He died Oct. 8. Two nurses who cared for him also, somehow, became infected; both have since been declared virus-free, October 8, 2014. (AP Photo/LM Otero, File)

They drew his blood, put tubes down his throat and wiped up his diarrhea. They analyzed his urine and wiped saliva from his lips, even after he had lost consciousness.

About 70 staff members at Texas Health Presbyterian Hospital were involved in the care of Thomas Eric Duncan after he was hospitalized, including a nurse now being treated for the same Ebola virus that killed the Liberian man who was visiting Dallas, according to medical records his family provided to The Associated Press.

The size of the medical team reflects the hospital's intense effort to save Duncan's life, but it also suggests that many other people could have been exposed to the virus during Duncan's time in an isolation unit.

On Monday, October 13, 2014 the director of the Centers for Disease Control and Prevention said the infection of the nurse means the agency must broaden the pool of people getting close monitoring. Authorities have said they do not know how 26-year-old nurse Nina Pham was infected, but they suspect some kind of breach in the hospital's protocol.

The medical records given to the AP offer clues, both to what happened and who was involved, but the hospital said the CDC does not have them.

A CDC spokeswoman said the agency reviewed the medical records with Duncan's care team and concluded that the documents were not helpful in identifying those who interacted directly with the patient.

"This is not something we can afford to experiment with. We need to get this right," said Ruth McDermott-Levy, who directs the Center for Global and Public Health in Villanova University's College of Nursing.

Until now, the CDC has been actively monitoring 48 people who might have had contact with Duncan after he fell ill with an infection but before he was put in isolation. The number included 10 people known to have contact and 38 who may have had contact, including people he was staying with and health care professionals who attended to him during an emergency room visit from which he was sent home. None is sick.

The CDC has not yet established a firm number of health care workers who had contact with Duncan.

"If this one individual was infected — and we don't know how — within the isolation unit, then it is possible that other individuals could have been infected as well," said Dr. Tom Frieden, director of the CDC. "We do not today have a number of such exposed people or potentially exposed health care workers. It's a relatively large number, we think in the end."

Caregivers who began treating Duncan after he tested positive for Ebola were following a "self-monitoring regimen" in which they were instructed to take their temperatures regularly and report any symptoms. But they were not considered at high risk. Pham went to the hospital Friday night after she took her temperature and found she had a fever.

Typically, the nurses, doctors and technicians caring for a contagious patient in isolation would be treating other people as well, and going home to their families after decontaminating themselves. The hospital has refused to answer questions about their specific duties.

The 1,400-plus pages of medical records show that nurses, doctors and other hospital employees wore face shields, double gowns, protective footwear and even hazmat suits to avoid touching any of Duncan's bodily fluids. Ebola spreads through direct contact with those fluids, usually blood, feces and vomit. The virus has also been detected in urine, semen and breast milk, and it may be in saliva and tears.

CDC officials said there were gaps in that protection at Texas Presbyterian, but they have not identified them and are investigating.

"Patient had large, extremely watery diarrhea," a nurse wrote in a report filed the day Duncan tested positive.

Another nurse noted that Duncan's urine was "darker in color with noted blood streaks."

It was unclear from the records released to the AP how many of the approximately 70 individuals involved in Duncan's care had direct contact with his body or fluids.

Dr. Aileen Marty, a World Health Organization doctor who recently returned to Florida International University after a month fighting Ebola in Nigeria, said no amount of protection is going to help if hospital workers do not put on and take off their protective layers carefully.

"The first thing in caring for someone with Ebola is to do everything in your power to never become a victim," she said.

And tracking all contacts, even within the medical setting, is complicated.

Generally, the first step in locating care providers for isolated infected patients is a personnel log on the door, "that should have everyone going in and out, signing in and out," said Dr. Lisa Esolen, Geisinger Health System's Medical Director of Health Services and Infection Prevention and Control. Medical records indicate the Dallas hospital had a log.

On the day before Duncan died, records indicate that at least nine caregivers entered and exited the room.

A spokesman for Texas Health Resources, the hospital's parent company, said the CDC probably has a log from the room door that would list everyone who got close to Duncan.

Dr. Christopher Ohl, who heads Wake Forest Baptist Medical Center's infectious-disease department and has worked with the CDC in the past, said the expanding monitoring "is an abundance of caution that's probably beyond what needs to be done" because medical caregivers will notice if they're getting a fever, and they're not contagious until that point.

"You start to know when you get those body aches and headaches, most people know that," he said. "It's not like you're surprised by it. Most people can figure out what to do when that happens."

Fear
Washington
October 23, 2014
By Seth Borenstein

Ebola is giving Americans a crash course in fear.

Yet, they're incredibly less likely to get the disease than to get sick worrying about it.

First, the reality check: More Americans have married Kim Kardashian — three — than contracted Ebola in the U.S. The two Dallas nurses who came down with Ebola were infected while treating a Liberian man, who became infected in West Africa. The New York doctor who has tested positive for Ebola had been treating people in West Africa.

Still, schools have been closed, people shunned and members of Congress have demanded travel bans and other dramatic action — even though health officials keep stressing that the disease is only spread through direct contact with bodily fluids from an infected person, and the risk to Americans is extremely low.

That's because Ebola pushes every fear button in our instincts, making us react more emotionally than rationally, experts say.

Three children on their way home from school stop to peer through the gate down at a building at The Ivy Apartments in Dallas where a man was diagnosed with having the Ebola virus was staying with family at the complex. Ebola is giving Americans a crash course in fear. Yet, they're incredibly less likely to get the disease than to get sick worrying about it, October 2, 2014. (AP Photo/Tony Gutierrez, File)

"The worry that people are being subjected to as a result of the hysteria around this is probably doing more damage than the actual disease," said E. Alison Holman, a professor at the University of California, Irvine, who studied the health effects of populations worried after watching coverage of the Sept. 11 attacks, the Boston Marathon bombing and Iraq war. "Frankly flu is more serious."

## THE IMPACT OF FEAR

Holman found in studies published by the American Medical Association that the people who spent more time watching television coverage on the Sept. 11 attacks — and reported fear and anxiety — were three times as likely to report new heart problems. The more coverage they watched, the more physical ailments they reported, she said.

Similarly, after the Boston Marathon bombing, people who watched six hours or more of coverage reported far more stress than those who watched less, Holman said. That was true even for those at the bombing.

Bruce McEwen, a neuroscientist who studies stress at Rockefeller University in New York, said the fear can lead people to change their lifestyle, making them isolate themselves, lose sleep, stop exercising, change their diet for the worse and drink or smoke.

"It's likely to cause them problems down the road even if there is no direct infection," McEwen said.

___

## GOOD FEAR VS. BAD FEAR

There are two types of fear that can almost come down to good fear and bad fear.

The good fear is the type we look for around Halloween in haunted houses or on roller coaster rides at amusement parks. It's short, intense, gets our juices going and removes boredom, said Vanderbilt University psychiatry professor David Zald.

"There's a benefit of being afraid. In controlled situations, many of us enjoy briefly being afraid," Zald said. "It can whip our attention to the here and now like nothing else."

There's a sense of mastery or bravery that comes out of walking out alive from a haunted house or giant roller coaster, Zald said.

That type of acute-but-short stress actually makes our immune system work better, McEwen said.

But long-term exposure to stress has the reverse effect on the immune system. That's when it elevates our blood pressure and contributes to heart disease.

___

## UNDERSTANDING THE RISK OF FEAR

One of the major unknown problems with risk and fear is that the public doesn't understand how at risk they are from worry, not disease. "It'll do far more damage than the disease," said David Ropeik, who teaches risk perception and communication and has written two books on risk.

Doctors and government officials tell us not to worry and how hard it is to get Ebola, which is re-assuring, Ropeik said. But "all the alarms are filling up on our radar screens," and we give more weight to the alarms because of the fear of death, he said.

Ebola pushes "all those fear buttons" because it is new and foreign, said George Gray, director of the Center for Risk Science and Public Health at George Washington University.

Part of it is just the fear of the unknown, said Mark Schuster, professor of pediatrics at Harvard Medical School. "It's not a name that's familiar. It doesn't sound like an English word. It comes from another continent."

Americans who say they don't quite understand how Ebola is transmitted report being more worried than those who say they do, according to an Associated Press-GfK Poll conducted in the past week and released Wednesday. Overall, 58 percent of those who acknowledge they don't understand Ebola very well say they are concerned it will spread widely in the U.S., compared to 46 percent of those who say they understand Ebola transmission.

We fear what we can't control. People often fear the far less deadly plane travel than driving because they aren't in control. Seeing trained medical professionals catch the disease despite protective gear only adds to the fear, Zald said.

Instead of using dry statistics such as 1 in 150 million, comparing your chances of contracting Ebola in America to that of marrying Kim Kardashian helps people understand and visualize risk better, Zald and Schuster said.

Mistakes and wrong statements by public health officials and politicization of the issue only make fear and public trust worse, said Baruch Fischhoff, a professor of decision sciences at Carnegie Mellon University.

Add wall-to-wall coverage that makes Ebola easy to picture.

"You create this hysteria about Ebola and unfounded fear, and people get all worried," Holman said.

Ropeik said, thinking about how worrying can make us sick may put Ebola more in perspective: "We need to fear the danger of getting risk wrong ... Chronic worry is really bad for our health."

Health officials are scrambling to begin human testing of a handful of experimental drugs for Ebola. But the effort has sparked an ethical debate over how to study unproven medicines amid an outbreak that has killed nearly 5,000.

# The Ethics of Drug Testing
## Washington
### November 12, 2014
### By Matthew Perrone

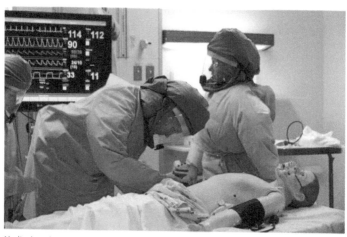

Medical workers wearing protective equipment surround and monitor a simulated patient during a demonstration for media members on their training for working with possible Ebola patients, at Madigan Army Medical Center on Joint Base Lewis McChord, near Tacoma, Wash, November 6, 2014. (AP Photo/Elaine Thompson)

U.S. officials say the studies must include one critical feature of traditional medical testing: a control group of patients who do not receive the drugs.

But many European and African authorities argue that withholding drugs from study participants is unethical, given that the current outbreak kills between 50 and 80 percent of those infected in West Africa, according to Doctors Without Borders. They favor alternative studies in which every patient receives drug therapy.

The split in testing philosophies means different researchers may wind up testing the same drugs using different approaches.

While there are no established drugs for Ebola, the Food and Drug Administration has allowed the emergency use of several experimental ones in U.S. patients. But agency officials say it's impossible to tell what affect the drugs have because patients in the U.S. also receive aggressive medical care, including fluid replacement, oxygen therapy and antibiotics.

Comparing patients receiving drug therapy to patients who are not is a long-established testing technique considered the gold standard of medical research. Officials from the FDA and the National Institutes of Health say the Ebola trials must stick to this model to get an accurate picture of whether the therapies are safe and effective.

FDA officials laid out plans last week for a study that would randomly assign patients to receive one of several drugs or aggressive medical care. Researchers would regularly assess patients taking the drugs, with the aim of switching over patients from the control group if one drug appears effective.

Dr. Luciana Borio, the FDA's director for counterterrorism and emerging threats, said she understands the ethical concerns associated with the approach.

"People do not like the idea of not receiving something that they think might help them, even though the fact is that we do not know yet if this stuff is going to help or hurt," Borio said.

FDA plans is to begin testing the approach on Ebola patients brought to the U.S. and then transfer the model over to Africa, where an estimated 13,270 people are infected.

U.S. medical ethicists tend to agree with the approach.

"It would be terrible to have a drug that we thought would work and offer it to these poor, suffering, and desperate people only to find out later— because we screwed up the clinical trials — that we were wrong," said Dr. Philip Rosoff, a professor of bioethics at Duke University.

But a coalition including Doctors without Borders, Oxford University and the French National Institute of Health and Medical Research plans to announce a study on Thursday that will give experimental drug therapy to all patients enrolled. Organizers say the current outbreak is so deadly that patients should have access to medicines that can potentially help them — even if their safety and effectiveness is uncertain.

"We have chosen this design because we think that it's not ethical to randomize patients to standard care in the conditions where these studies are conducted," said Piero Olliaro, an Oxford University professor and WHO official.

Under the study plan, researchers will measure the death rate of Ebola patients given an experimental drug over two weeks. If the mortality rate falls as low as 20 percent, researchers say they will know they have an effective treatment.

Similar trial designs are sometimes used to study deadly forms of cancer for which there are no established treatments. In the 1980s, some of the earliest HIV drugs were also tested in trials where all patients received drug therapy. But at the time AIDS was a fatal disease with no known cure. Ebola, on the other hand, is well understood and can be cured via traditional medical care.

Olliaro said he could not name the drug that would be used in the European study, but he pointed out that the WHO has outlined several drugs that could be suitable for study in Africa, including antiviral pills from Chimerix and BioCryst Pharmaceuticals. Both of those drugs are designed to block enzymes that allow viruses to reproduce, though they have not yet been tested specifically against Ebola.

A WHO report released last week attempted to find consensus among researchers, stating that all testing methodologies should be considered ethical. However, the report notes that officials from Guinea and Liberia said that randomized, controlled trials "would not be acceptable to local communities."

Additionally, the report states that cultural and ethical factors could make it difficult to obtain permission for randomized studies in Africa.

For now, Olliaro says officials must move past ethical debates and begin testing, regardless of the method.

"I think it's high time to stop discussing and start acting," he said.

### 80 to 100 Cases Per Day
United Nations
December 5, 2014
By Edith M. Lederer

Sierra Leone said Friday, December 5, 2014 that between 80 and 100 new cases of Ebola are being reported every day and the country now hardest-hit by the deadly virus desperately needs over 1,000 beds to treat victims.

Sierra Leone's Finance Minister Kaifalah Marah painted a grim picture to the U.N. Economic and Social Council Friday of the challenges facing his West African nation which failed to meet a World Health Organization interim goal of isolating 70 percent of Ebola patients and safely burying 70 percent of victims by Dec. 1.

The two other hard-hit countries, Liberia and Guinea, did meet the deadline, and the U.N.'s Ebola chief Dr. David Nabarro said the number of new cases in Liberia has dropped from 60 per day in September to 10 per day now.

But Nabarro and WHO Director-General Dr. Margaret Chan stressed that Ebola that a much greater effort is needed to reach the elusive goal of zero new cases.

"The Ebola outbreak is the largest, longest, most severe and most complex Ebola epidemic in the nearly 40-year history of this disease," Chan said. "What began as a health crisis has become a crisis with humanitarian, social, economic and security implications."

Kissi Dembadouno sits in his home in the Guinean village of Meliandou, some 400 miles (600 kms) south-east of Conakry, Guinea. Demnadouno lost his wife, daughter and two grandchildren to the deadly disease. He is Etienne Ouamouno's father in law. Etienne Ouamouno's 2-year old son Emile is widely recognized by researchers as Patient Zero, the first person to have died of Ebola back on December 28 last year. And Meliandou, a small village at the top of a forested hill reached by a rutted red earth track, is notorious as the birthplace and crucible of the most deadly incarnation of the virus to date, November 20, 2014. (AP Photo/Jerome Delay)

She said by videoconference from Geneva that "the fear for Ebola is moving faster than the virus."

Marah said as of Thursday there were 6,201 confirmed Ebola cases in Sierra Leone and 1,900 deaths, and the virus is now concentrated in some northern districts and the western area including the capital, Freetown.

Sierra Leone has four functioning treatment centers but it needs 12, and while the number of beds for Ebola sufferers has increased from 212 to 406 it needs 1,500 — which means 1,094 additional beds, he said.

Marah said Sierra Leone also needs 6,000 people to scale-up the tracing of contacts of Ebola victims.

Chan said clinical trials for an Ebola vaccine "look promising," and experimental therapies including some potential cures are also undergoing clinical trials.

"Most experts are convinced that this will not be Africa's last Ebola outbreak," Chan said. "At least 22 African countries ... have the ecological conditions, the wildlife species, and the hunting practices that favor a return of Ebola at some time in the future."

## A Hard Lesson to Learn
Dakar, Senegal
January 24, 2015
By Krista Larson

A top U.N. official in the fight against Ebola greeted just three patients at one treatment center he visited this week in Sierra Leone. Families in Liberia are no longer required to cremate the remains of loved ones to halt the spread of the virulent disease.

And in the streets of Guinea's capital, it is rare to see the formerly ubiquitous plastic buckets of bleach and water for hand washing.

Ten months after it dawned on health officials that they were facing an unprecedented Ebola outbreak in West Africa, experts and officials agree the tide is turning, although previous lulls have proved short-lived.

There is still no vaccine or licensed treatment, nor is it clear whether the international community has actually learned any lessons from an epidemic that killed at least 8,675 people.

"Things have changed drastically for the better — no one can deny that," said Aitor Sanchez Lacomba, Liberia country director for the International Rescue Committee. "How can we make sure that we don't have these kinds of situations in the future?"

Previous disease outbreaks, including SARS and bird flu, prompted calls to build strong health surveillance systems and to reinforce agencies like the World Health Organization. But little has changed.

A child, center, stands underneath a signboard as a family home is placed under quarantine due to the Ebola virus in Port Loko, Sierra Leone, October 22, 2014. (AP Photo/Michael Duff, File)

After the 2009 swine flu pandemic, WHO commissioned an independent review, which recommended creating a $100 million emergency fund for health crises and beefing up rapid-response health experts. Neither has been done.

The human toll of Ebola can be starkly seen in one plot of land in Liberia's capital where only Ebola victims are buried now. Cards placed on sticks and stuck into the ground carry the names of those who died. One day, families hope they will be replaced with concrete gravestones marking the years of birth and death as sunrise and sunset.

"Recriminations are counterproductive, but it will be necessary to understand whether this outbreak could have been responded to quicker with less cost and less suffering," U.N. Ebola chief, Dr. David Nabarro, told the U.N. General Assembly earlier this week.

Julius Kamara, a father to two girls who remain home instead of going to school, said sometimes the plastic buckets in Sierra Leone's capital for handwashing are now empty. There are fewer checkpoints, restrictions on movements are being lifted but gatherings are banned and bars and clubs are closed.

"We are all looking forward to when life can get back to normal," he said. Sierra Leone plans to reopen schools in March, following Guinea which opened them this week. Liberia is set to reopen schools on Feb. 2.

"The epidemic has turned," Ismael Ould Cheikh Ahmed, the new head of the U.N. Mission for Ebola Emergency Response known as UNMEER, recently declared. The number of cases in Guinea and Sierra Leone is at its lowest since August, and in Liberia it's the lowest since June.

Still, he and other officials caution that they lack critical information about the cases that do remain. Only about half of new cases in Guinea and Liberia are from known contacts, meaning that the remainder is getting infected from unknown sources.

No such statistics even exist for Sierra Leone, where deaths are still being underreported because families want to carry out burials in accordance with tradition, which involves touching bodies — one of the quickest ways to spread Ebola.

"There are still numbers of new cases that are alarming, and there are hotspots that are emerging in new places that make me believe there is still quite a lot of the disease that we're not seeing," said Nabarro, the U.N. Ebola chief.

The outbreak has not killed as many people as some predictions. At its height, one estimate warned that as many as 1.4 million people could become infected by mid-January if there were no additional interventions. Instead, the probable, suspected and confirmed case toll is 21,797 with 8,675 deaths.

———

Nearly every agency and government stumbled in its response to Ebola, now expected to cost the three most-affected countries at least $1.6 billion in lost economic growth in 2015.

In an internal draft document obtained by The Associated Press last year, WHO acknowledged there was "a failure to see that conditions for explosive spread were present right at the start."

WHO blamed incompetent staff and said it let bureaucratic bungles delay people and money to fight the virus. The document said the agency was hampered by budget cuts and the need to battle other diseases flaring around the world.

"We're always looking to improve and we want to do better next time, so we will listen to what our member states have to say," said WHO spokesman Gregory Hartl.

Brice de le Vingne, director of operations for Doctors Without Borders, said the Ebola outbreak exposed a vacuum in global health leadership.

"The world today doesn't have a proper organization to respond quickly to this kind of catastrophe," he said.

Officials must also think about changing risky cultural practices in future epidemics, said Dr. Peter Piot, director of the London School of Hygiene and Tropical Medicine and co-discoverer of the Ebola virus.

"I think we underestimate how incredibly difficult it is to change behavior," he told AP. "We make guidelines about it, but there is so much more to it than that."

Health officials also agree that time was wasted on nearly every aspect of the Ebola response. It took too long to build treatment centers. The countries that sent soldiers to West Africa — namely Britain and the U.S. — did not fully commit to the effort, said De le Vingne. Still, he is optimistic the un-precedented scale of the Ebola outbreak will prompt change, and that future outbreaks will be detected more quickly.

On Sunday, WHO's executive board plans to discuss several proposals that could redefine how the U.N. health agency responds to outbreaks. In a re-cent report, WHO wondered if the commitment to battling the dreaded disease will remain strong.

"The virus has demonstrated its tenacity time and time again," the report said. "Will national and international control efforts show an equally tena-cious staying power?"

# 11

# Ebola Then and Now

A health official takes temperature of a soccer fan for Ebola Virus ahead of the African Cup of Nations Group D soccer match between Ivory Coast and Guinea at the Estadio De Malabo, Equatorial Guinea, January 20, 2015. (AP Photo/Sunday Alamba)

A Different Ebola from 25 Years Ago
Reston, Virginia
August 10, 2014
By Matthew Barakat,

It had all the makings of a public-health horror story: an outbreak of a wildly deadly virus on the doorstep of the nation's capital, with dozens of lab monkeys dead, multiple people testing positive, and no precedent in this country on how to contain it.

Americans' introduction to the Ebola virus came 25 years ago in an office park near Washington Dulles International Airport, a covert crisis that captivated the public only years later when it formed the basis of a bestselling book.

Initially thought to be the same hyper-deadly strain as the current Ebola outbreak that has killed hundreds in Africa, the previously unknown Reston variant turned out to be nonlethal to humans. But the story of what might have been illustrates how far U.S. scientists have come in their understanding of a virus whose very name strikes fear, even in a country where no one has fatally contracted it.

Gerald Jaax, one of the leaders of a team of Army scientists that responded to the 1989 outbreak in Reston, Virginia, closely watched the meticulously planned transfers this month of two American aid workers from Liberia to a specialized facility in Atlanta, the first Ebola patients ever brought to the U.S. Jaax recalled his days urgently trying to corral the country's first known outbreak.

In the fall of 1989, dozens of macaques imported from the Philippines suddenly died at Hazelton Research Products' primate quarantine unit in Reston, where animals were kept and later sold for lab testing. Company officials contacted the U.S. Army Medical Research Institute of Infectious Diseases at Fort Detrick, Maryland — Jaax's unit — concerned they might be dealing with an outbreak of hemorrhagic fever among the monkeys.

Initial testing revealed something much worse: Ebola, specifically the Zaire strain, which had a 90 percent fatality rate in humans. Four workers at the quarantine facility tested positive for exposure to the virus.

Amazingly, they never even got sick.

Researchers eventually realized they were dealing with a different strain, one now known as Ebola-Reston. Though its appearance under a microscope is similar to the Zaire strain, Ebola-Reston is the only one of the five forms of Ebola not harmful to humans.

But Jaax and his unit, including his wife Nancy , also a scientist, did not know that while at the monkey house. They just knew they had to clean it out, and do it while keeping a relatively low profile that wouldn't scare the neighbors.

"You could walk in and smell monkey everywhere," said Dr. C.J. Peters, who oversaw the Army's response to the outbreak. "There was a little shopping center nearby. ... There was plenty of opportunity for trouble."

While the Army scientists had strong protocols in place for studying viruses safely in a lab, they were not well prepared to stabilize and contain an outbreak in a private facility. At the time, Jaax said, nobody — including the U.S. Centers for Disease Control — had that kind of experience. In the Reston incident, the CDC took the lead in managing the human-health aspect of the response, while the Army dealt with the monkeys.

Back in 1989, there was concern that Ebola could spread through the air, said Peters, now a professor with University of Texas Medical Branch in Galveston. Indeed, researchers concluded there must have been some sort of aerosol spread of the virus within the monkey house, Jaax said.

The Reston animals had to be euthanized from a safe distance — "monkeys are aerosol-producing machines," Jaax said. In his 1995 book "The Hot Zone," Richard Preston described how Jaax modified a mop handle so it could be used to pin a monkey in its cage where it could safely be injected and eventually euthanized. Later, to disinfect the air, the team cooked formaldehyde crystals on electric frying pans.

Ebola is no longer thought to be an airborne virus; scientists say the disease can only be spread through direct contact with bodily fluids.

The Reston crisis also elevated Ebola into the public consciousness, albeit not immediately. In an era when the country was preoccupied with the AIDS epidemic, which hit 100,000 cases in the U.S. that year, the Army and CDC scientists carried out their tasks in relative obscurity.

It was only after "The Hot Zone" became a best-seller and focused attention on the public-health battle to confront emerging disease outbreaks that the Reston event became well known and Ebola became a household word.

"The big difference between now and 1989 is that nobody else knew what Ebola was," said Jaax, now an associate vice president at Kansas State University.

One of the most important legacies of Reston, Jaax said, was that none of the dozens who worked to contain the outbreak was exposed to the virus. The plans developed on the fly to keep the responders safe worked, he said, and provided a good blueprint for the protocols used to bring back the American aid workers earlier this month.

Dr. Amesh Adalja, senior associate at the UPMC Center for Health Security in Baltimore and an infectious disease physician, said the Reston responders' incorrect belief that they were dealing with a virus that was deadly to humans provided the ideal trial run for handling such an outbreak.

"It's like you're performing with a net underneath you, but you don't know it's a drill," Adalja said.

Ebola-Reston returned to the U.S. in 1996 in monkeys in Texas that had been imported from the Philippines. The Philippines has seen three outbreaks since the strain was identified, affecting primates, pigs and nine people. The workers who handled the animals developed antibodies, but did not get sick.

Hazelton abandoned the Reston facility in 1990, and the company was later swallowed up by a competitor. The monkey house was torn down a few years later. The new building there hosts several small offices and a day-care center.

Some of the office park workers are aware of the site's history; many are not.

Back in 1989, Vicky Wingert worked at the local homeowners' association, in offices across the street from the monkey house. She said nobody had any idea there was a problem until people showed up in hazmat suits. Even then, very little information trickled out, she said.

"At the time, it wasn't a big deal. Looking back, it probably should have been," she said.

Ostracized
Monrovia, Liberia
October 9, 2014
By Krista Larson

First 16-year-old Promise Cooper's mother complained of a hurting head and raging fever, and she died days later on the way to the hospital. The following month, her father developed the same headache and fever. Her baby brother grew listless and sick too, and refused to take a bottle. That's when Promise knew this was not malaria.

She had heard about Ebola on the radio. When she tended to her father, she washed her hands immediately afterward. Desperate to keep her three younger siblings safe, she urged them to play outside their one-room home. Yet she was powerless before an invisible enemy, as her family of seven disintegrated around her.

In the meantime, neighbors and relatives were starting to become suspicious. No one came by to check on the kids, not even their grandparents. Word, like the virus, was spreading through Liberia's capital: The Coopers had Ebola.

A child selling clothes waits for customers in the St Paul's Bridge neighborhood of Monrovia, Liberia, September 26, 2014. (AP Photo/Jerome Delay)

In Liberia's large, deeply religious families, there is usually an aunty somewhere willing to take in a child who has lost a parent. But Ebola, and the fear of contagion and death, is now unraveling bonds that have lasted for generations.

At least 3,700 children across Liberia, Guinea and Sierra Leone have lost one or more parents to Ebola, according to the U.N. children's agency, and that figure is expected to double by mid-October. Many of these children are left to fend for themselves, and continue to live inside infected houses.

Promise was used to looking after her younger siblings, and often carried a baby cousin on her hip around the neighborhood. When her mother was alive, they would alternate weeks of cooking. She knew how to make porridge for breakfast, rice with potato greens for dinner.

When her father fell sick, she took over all the things her mother used to do. There was no school because of the Ebola epidemic, so she had time to wash her brothers' soccer jerseys and jeans.

But nothing she did could help 5-month-old Success, whose name reflected his parents' dreams. Just like their mother, the little boy died. There was nobody to help them and no ambulance to spare, so his body stayed in the house for several days.

By the time the ambulance finally came to take away her father and the tiny corpse bundled in blankets, 11-year-old Emmanuel Jr. was stricken too.

Promise watched as medics packed half her family into the back of the ambulance. She was now alone with 15-year-old Benson and 13-year-old Ruth.

She could not afford a phone call to see how their father and brother were doing, even if she could get through on the hotline for relatives that was almost always busy. A taxi to the Ebola clinic across town cost even more. An uncle stopped by to drop off some money, but left without touching the children for fear of infection.

Promise resolved to keep the family together until her father came back.

She decided to use what little cash she had to buy plastic bags of drinking water. The family had a cooler, and she planned to sell the bags she bought at $1 apiece for $2.

Day after day, though, no customers came. Nobody wanted to buy water from the girl whose mother died of Ebola, and whose father and brother were at the clinic. Promise looked healthy, but fear was overcoming compassion in the St. Paul Bridge neighborhood where they lived.

If the children sat down somewhere, people would spray bleach after they got up. When they tried to buy something with what little money they had, vendors refused to serve them.

Neighbors didn't want the Cooper boys playing with their children. And even though health workers had disinfected the path from the well that went right past their house, women took their brightly colored plastic buckets the long way around instead.

Promise, overcome with grief and beaten down by stigma, became depressed.

"Why don't you want to talk to me? Why God does nobody want to come around?" she sobbed. "We are human beings."

―――

Finally she scraped together enough change from a cousin to take a taxi to the gates of the Ebola clinic. A security guard said he would check whether Emmanuel Cooper Sr. was on the list of the living.

Promise and Ruth paced outside the barbed-wire topped walls of the clinic for what felt like hours, waiting for an answer on when he would be coming home.

The guard came back. He said he was sorry, but their father was dead.

The girls broke down sobbing.

No one could tell them if 11-year-old Emmanuel was still alive.

————

Even as Promise lost both her parents, another man in the community was trying to document just how many children were orphaned in the St. Paul Bridge community. Kanyean Molton Farley, a human rights researcher by day, devoted all his spare time to making a list of the now 28 parentless children living alone. In most cases, teenagers like Promise are now raising their siblings amid an overwhelmed social welfare system.

"The story of the Cooper children touched my gut, and I never stopped coming back," he said one morning, as he dropped off soap for the children.

The family's rent was already paid through the end of the year, but they soon ran out of money to pay the electricity. Farley worried most of all that Promise could fall prey to an older man. At 16 and hungry, she was vulnerable to abuse.

Then the Cooper children caught a lucky break: Promise saw her brother's face on television, among government photos of children who had survived Ebola at the city's clinics but were still separated from their families.

"It's him, it's him!" she told Farley. Off they went to get Emmanuel — the first in the family to survive the plague sweeping their neighborhood.

Not long after Emmanuel came home, Ruth became feverish and unwell one night. How could this be happening again? A terrified Promise called their friend Farley late at night. He couldn't come until morning because of the curfew.

So he told her to use the family's mattresses as room dividers in the single bedroom where they all slept. Ruth would stay on one side; the healthy children would sleep on the other.

At first light, an ambulance called by Farley took Ruth to the hospital.

————

Now it is just Promise and the boys.

She insists they will never go live with strangers. Yet they no longer want to stay in the house where their parents lay dying and their brother's body sat for days.

On a Sunday afternoon after church, there is no television to watch without electricity. The TV set sits gathering dust with a soiled stuffed unicorn on top of it.

The children sleep together in their parents' bed at night, instead of crowding on the floor below as they did in their previous life. Some nights her brothers weep for their mother, and Promise tries to be firm but caring.

"I tell them Ma and Pa are no more, and that they shouldn't worry about that," she says. "We must concentrate on living our lives because they are gone."

Just a few weeks ago, their aunt Helen came around to the house — the first family member to do so in months. She had been upcountry when the children's parents died and wanted to see how they were doing. It pains her to think of her brother, and what he would say about the children out of school, cooking and cleaning for themselves.

"I have to come back because everyone has abandoned them," says Helen Kangbo, breast-feeding her 1-year-old daughter Faith after joining her nieces and nephews for a paltry dinner of rice. "I must have the courage to come." Of course, now that Helen is in contact with the children, she is shunned by the same extended family that fears Promise and her siblings.

Each day Promise mixes up bleach and water in bottles to keep the house and her brothers clean. "Don't go around people. Don't touch your friends. Anything you touch, you wash your hands," she scolds them.

Days later, she says her prayers have been answered: After three weeks at an Ebola treatment center, 13-year-old Ruth is cured. She is still weak, so she is staying with Farley's family. When Ruth is well enough she will return home.

Here in their house, there is little trace left of dead loved ones, because authorities have burned their parents' clothing in a bid to stop the spread of the disease. The only photos of their parents are on their voter ID cards. And the only reminder of Success is the two bottles of baby powder, still sitting on a table in the room.

# Ebola Through the Lens

# Photos by Jerome Delay

Kissi Dembadouno, center, is comforted by relatives outside his home in the Guinean village of Meliandou, some 400 miles (600 kms) south-east of Conakry, Guinea, believed to be Ebola's ground zero. Demnadouno lost his wife, daughter and two grandchildren to the deadly disease. He is Etienne Ouamouno's father in law. The first reported case of Ebola is Etienne's son, Emile, who passed away late December 2013, November 20, 2014. (AP Photo/Jerome Delay)

The list of Ebola victims in the Guinean village of Meliandou, some 400 miles (600 mms) south-east of Conakry, Guinea, believed to be Ebola's ground zero. Meliandou, a small village at the top of a forested hill reached by a rutted red earth track, is notorious as the birthplace and crucible of the most deadly incarnation of the Ebola virus to date. Today villagers here are in debt, stigmatized, hungry and still angry and deeply suspicious about who or what brought the disease that has devastated their lives, November 20, 2014. (AP Photo/Jerome Delay)

Children listen to the village chief in the communal room in the Guinean village of Meliandou, some 400 miles (600 mms) south-east of Conakry, Guinea, believed to be Ebola's ground zero. Meliandou, a small village at the top of a forested hill reached by a rutted red earth track, is notorious as the birthplace and crucible of the most deadly incarnation of the Ebola virus to date. Today villagers here are in debt, stigmatized, hungry and still angry and deeply suspicious about who or what brought the disease that has devastated their lives, November 20, 2014. (AP Photo/Jerome Delay)

A child grabs food from a woman in the Guinean village of Meliandou, some 400 miles (600 kms) south-east of Conakry, Guinea, believed to be Ebola's ground zero. The official theory is that somehow the virus was transmitted from fruit bats to humans and spread through the region plagued with bad roads, dense population, and a problematic health care system along a porous borders that people used to cross regularly –before the outbreak—whether to join family or engage in trade, November 23, 2014. (AP Photo/Jerome Delay)

A women gather in the Guinean village of Meliandou, some 400 miles (600 kms) south-east of Conakry, Guinea, believed to be Ebola's ground zero. In Meliandou, as in many other villages across Ebola country, the disease is shrouded in mystery, surrounded by suspicion and rumors. People here still believe that Ebola was disseminated by white people seeking the deaths of blacks, including through a measles vaccination campaign; by a laboratory testing bats to create a vaccination against the virus; by politicians from a rival tribe bent on killing off the forest people; by white miners looking to exploit a nearby mountain of iron ore, November 23, 2014. (AP Photo/Jerome Delay)

Young girls return from the water well in the Guinean village of Meliandou, some 400 miles (600 kms) south-east of Conakry, Guinea, believed to be Ebola's ground zero. Village chief Amadou Kamano, fearing that the entire village was cursed, said people from other villages blamed Meliandou for bringing the deaths and, at one point, blocked their access to the only road to the main road and to the water well, November 23, 2014. (AP Photo/Jerome Delay)

Esther David, 17, sits in the room she and her sister share at their uncle's house in the St Paul's Bridge neighborhood of Monrovia, Liberia. Esther, a single mother herself, lost both parents to the Ebola Virus, September 26, 2014. (AP Photo/Jerome Delay)

John Tamba, 17, stands in his uncle's house in the St Paul's Bridge neighborhood of Monrovia, Liberia. John lost both parents to the Ebola Virus, September 26, 2014. (AP Photo/Jerome Delay)

Bystanders react as they listen to a street preacher calling on people to raise their hands and "Wave Ebola Bye Bye" in Monrovia, Liberia, September 27, 2014. (AP Photo/Jerome Delay)

# Questions Answered

Ebola 101 from the AP
Washington
July 4, 2014
By The Associated Press

Hospitals are being urged to be more vigilant in watching for travelers with Ebola.

## WHEN IS EBOLA CONTAGIOUS?

Only when someone is showing symptoms, which can start with vague symptoms including a fever, flu-like body aches and abdominal pain, and then vomiting and diarrhea.

## HOW DOES EBOLA SPREAD?

Through close contact with a symptomatic person's bodily fluids, such as blood, sweat, vomit, feces, urine, saliva or semen. Those fluids must have an entry point, like a cut or scrape or someone touching the nose, mouth or eyes with contaminated hands, or being splashed. That's why health care workers wear protective gloves and other equipment.

## WHAT ABOUT MORE CASUAL CONTACT?

Ebola isn't airborne. "If you sit next to someone on the bus, you're not exposed," said Dr. Tom Frieden, director of the Centers for Disease Control and Prevention.

"This is not like flu. It's not like measles, not like the common cold. It's not as spreadable, it's not as infectious as those conditions," he added.

## WHO GETS TESTED WHEN EBOLA IS SUSPECTED?

Hospitals with a suspected case call their health department or the CDC to go through a checklist to determine the person's level of risk. Among the questions are whether the person reports a risky contact with a known Ebola patient, how sick they are and whether an alternative diagnosis is more likely. Most initially suspicious cases in the U.S. haven't met the criteria for testing.

## HOW IS IT CLEANED UP?

The CDC says bleach and other hospital disinfectants kill Ebola. Dried virus on surfaces survives only for several hours.

# THE AP EMERGENCY RELIEF FUND

When Hurricane Katrina hit the Gulf Coast in 2005, many Associated Press staffers and their families were personally affected. AP employees rallied to help these colleagues by setting up the AP Emergency Relief Fund, which has since become a source of crucial assistance worldwide to AP staff and their families who have suffered damage or loss as a result of conflict or natural disasters.

Established as an independent 501(c)(3), the Fund provides a quick infusion of cash to help staff and their families rebuild homes, relocate and repair and replace damaged possessions.

The AP donates the net proceeds from AP Essentials, AP's company store, to the Fund.

## HOW TO GIVE

In order to be ready to help the moment emergencies strike, the Fund relies on the generous and ongoing support of the extended AP community. Donations can be made any time at http://www.ap.org/relieffund and are tax deductible.

On behalf of the AP staffers and families who receive aid in times of crisis, the AP Emergency Relief Fund Directors and Officers thank you.

# ALSO AVAILABLE FROM AP EDITIONS

**MUHAMMAD ALI**
Athlete of the Century

**GAY AMERICA**
The Road to Gay Marriage and LGBT Rights

**CHRISTIANS UNDER ATTACK**
Struggles and Persecution Throughout the World

**THE HUBBLE SPACE TELESCOPE**
A Decade of Data Discovery

**THE COLLAPSE OF THE SOVIET UNION**
Rise of an Empire

**WARREN BUFFETT**
The Oracle of Omaha

**MARIJUANA NATION**
The Legalization of Cannabis Across the West

**EBOLA**
Major Outbreaks in Times to Understand

**PEARL HARBOR**
Day of Infamy

CPSIA information can be obtained at www.ICGtesting.com
Printed in the USA
LVOW02s1436270215

428649LV00033B/183/P